REMEMBRANCES

of

Rev. Thomas Williamson Hooper, D.D.
Joseph Richardson Haw
Mary Jane Haw

Hanover County, Virginia

Compiled and Edited by
Arthur Hastings Taylor, III

Front Cover: *Examining Illustrations by the Fire,* **by** Edward Lamson Henry (1872), public domain

All correspondence and inquires should be directed to:
Arthur H. Taylor, III
15548 Tyler Station Road
Beaverdam, VA 23015-1413

Printed in the United States of America

Dedication

To my Mother
Ann Hooper Call Taylor

Whose love of family and family history gave me life, the spirit and dedication to find out, "**Who I am, where I came from and how I got here.**" and to share this interest with family and others. ...and she was so very proud that her given name contained the surname Hooper, the only one so named in her family.

Ann Hooper Call Taylor
Born: 7 Jan 1921, Richmond, VA,
Stuart Circle Hospital
Married: 1 Oct 1942
Rocky Mount, NC,
Arthur Hastings Taylor Jr., M.D.
Died: 26 Sep 2004, Ashland, VA.

Daughter of George Wellford Call and Cleo Miles Hearon.
All are buried in Forest Lawn Cemetery

CONTENTS

Foreword

This compilation of articles by Dr. T. W. Hooper, Joseph R. Haw and Miss Mary J. Haw is of special interest and value to the present day as it tells first-hand of life in Hanover County before and immediately after the Civil War. As Hanover County is a "burned record county" with few records prior to 1865, these articles add greatly to the county's history.

The articles by Dr. Hooper tell first-hand of his life as a Hanover youth and his education in small plantation schools. He refers to his ministry at Polegreen Church, now a historic landmark site on Rural Point Road, and Beulah Presbyterian Church, where he describes its beginnings, its destruction, and its rebuilding.

The period to which he refers covers the years prior to the Civil War when Hanover was peaceful and a quiet countryside, with farming as its main source of income. Although Rev. Hooper had left the county before the outbreak of hostilities, he refers to the devastation afterward when he returned to visit to his old home.

The articles by Joseph R. Haw and his sister, Miss Mary J. Haw, refer to the Haw and Watt families and to the Studley/Haw's Shop area, Springfield (Farm) (Watt House) and the area during and after The Seven Days' Battle. This brother and sister further enhance and expand upon the Hooper characters, places and events.

In bringing these articles written almost one hundred years ago to the attention of present day citizens of Hanover, Art Taylor has contributed a valuable source of information found nowhere else.

The county, and its historical organizations, are grateful for his efforts in compiling a page of history on Hanover's past.

Helen K. Yates

Acknowledgements

What is interesting about this collection of articles is that other than in their original publications, most have not been republished in their entirety or in associated groups. In this endeavor, and considering that this effort began some twenty-five years ago, the articles, narratives on the homes and census information had to be retyped in much the old-fashioned way. The only force and means to this end was and is my wife, Dale Murphy Taylor, who typed almost every word, and for this I am most grateful and thankful. My keyboard speed would have me still typing today! (I still use the Columbus typing method... when I find it, I land on it.)

I am also grateful to Judy Lowry who edited and indexed the early manuscript. She serves as director of the Page Library of Local History & Genealogy, Editor of the *Hanover County Historical Society Bulletin*, and has published several books about Hanover County.

The Hanover County Historical Society has allowed the use of the text from *Old Homes of Hanover County, Virginia* for the homes identified in this publication.

John M. Gabbert has kindly allowed the use of maps from his book *Military Operations in Hanover County, Virginia 1861-1865*.

The Pamunkey Woman's Club, through Virginia Darnell, has graciously allowed the use of selected sketches from their annual calendars of old homes and other points of interest in Hanover County. These sketches are done by local artists for the calendar which is a fundraiser for the Club.

Louis Manarin has allowed the use of several pictures from his book *15ᵗʰ Virginia Infantry*.

A special acknowledgement is in order for the person who has set the standard for study of history and genealogy of Hanover County, Virginia, its publication and the love of it all. Helen Kay Yates is the epitome of all of this and is the inspiration for a great deal of my interest in history and genealogy of Hanover County. I strive to be as meticulous to detail and accuracy as I know she approves of nothing less. Everyone needs to learn and know this lesson. Her very kind *Foreword* is special and greatly appreciated.

Introduction

"...I know of no way of judging of the future but by the past."
Patrick Henry

These words by Patrick Henry in his speech to the Virginia Convention, Richmond, Virginia on March 23, 1775, were spoken in the name of freedom and our movement toward this basic entitlement. They also cause us to realize the importance of preserving our history and reflecting upon it.

Genealogy is an enjoyable and consuming hobby or avocation depending on one's point of view. Generally speaking, it is the study or tracing of one's ancestry and the assembly and compilation of these tracings. It fills in blanks, sheds light on "who we are, where we came from and how we got here." It is the study of the past and history by which we discover and judge ourselves.

Part of this "tracing" involves the reading, scanning and even committing to memory of anything and everything to do with families and history. (If this sudden interest in history at these generally "much past the required study days of school" could be channeled to those earlier "required" study of history years, we would be scholars of history and better judges of the future. But alas, it isn't to be! It is simply too late.)

Research has led me to the discovery and use of many obscure and little-used print mediums. Three of these are the *Richmond Dispatch* of 1895, the *Confederate Veteran Magazine* of 1925 and 1926 and the *Christian Observer* of 1910. These three diverse publications share several common elements beyond the obvious as print mediums. Not only do they contain invaluable historical and genealogical information, but they were the medium for three talented writers who were descended from the Haw family of Leeds, England and the Watt family of Glenarm, County Antrim, Ireland.

John Haw I settled in Hanover County in the Studley (Haw's Shop) area and Hugh Watt settled on the Chickahominy River at Springfield Farm (Watt House).

Descendants of these families played valuable roles in the development of Hanover County, and of the background and substance for these "first-hand account" articles. You will see the relationships of families and friends. You will recognize the names and stories of and about many other prominent families of this eastern part of Hanover.

These articles describe the life, times, people and events of the area from Cold Harbor to Haw's Shop community to the Courthouse. They even go beyond Hanover County to the Commonwealth of Virginia in general. Battles, politics, religion, sporting events and education are discussed in detail, often in such terms so as to be identified with the present. This is with respect to Patrick Henry's "past" and "future" reference.

Beginning in February 1895, Thomas Williamson Hooper, D. D. (1832-1915), a great grandson of John Haw I and prominent Presbyterian minister of Polegreen, Salem and Beulah Presbyterian Churches from 1857 to 1863, wrote six articles or reminiscences for the *Richmond Dispatch* newspaper. Exactly why he wrote these articles is not clear, but the results and insights provided are very clear.

The winter of 1894-95, according to the *Daily Dispatch* was severe, one of the most severe on record in terms of the freeze and snow accumulations. With weather of this nature, writing represented a good way to pass the time.

His accounts of growing up in Hanover County on Beaverdam Farm, going to school and later on to college at Hampden-Sidney [sic], ministering at Polegreen, Salem and Beulah Presbyterian Churches, etc., is "worth the price of admission." He ties together one and all and everything: families, individual characters, places, history, anecdotes, politics ... just about everything dealing with everyday life ... but some 160 years ago.

Reverend Hooper was a powerful writer as is evidenced by these articles. He was "schooled" well beyond what many considered typical at that time. His early education was well-rounded and was further honed at the college level. He was able to combine his command of the English language, religious training, character and personality into a creative writing style that was entertaining and informative. Imagine hearing him preach!

It is unfortunate only six articles are known or can be found, because you will want to read more and more and are sorry to finish the last. Slip back in time as you read and enjoy these articles.

In 1925, Joseph Richardson Haw (1845-1911) wrote two articles for the *Confederate Veteran Magazine*. A third article, "The Haw Boys in the War Between the States" appeared in the same volume and was probably written by him even though no credit is given. He also responded to an account of the Battle of First Cold Harbor in the 1926 *Confederate Veteran Magazine*.

Mr. Haw was the great grandson of John Haw I and grandson of Hugh Watt. He was a Confederate veteran of Hanover County and ultimately lived and died in the Hampton, Virginia area. Like many veterans, he wrote articles for the *Veteran* and seems to have been active in this arena.

His articles describe the Haw family, their contributions and experiences in the Civil War, and an account of the fighting in and around the Haw's Shop area on May 28, 1864. The article about the Haw's Shop community lends support to the Hooper articles, expanding upon and describing many of the same families, events, etc., and at the same time introducing others.

Miss Mary Jane Haw (1835-1927), sister of Joseph R. Haw, wrote an article which appeared in the *Christian Observer* in 1910. She was an active writer of her time, having also written several novels — *The Beechwood Tragedy, A Tale of the Chickahominy* and *The Rivals: A Chickahominy Story.*

Both brother and sister Haw's articles are first-hand accounts of family related events as well as of the same nature and significance as Reverend Hooper's recollections. An interesting perspective in the Haw articles is in the time immediately preceding and leading into The Seven Days' Battle at the Watt House on June 27, 1862.

Mr. Haw describes being camped across the Chickahominy River from the Watt House and being so near to family while Miss Haw describes being able to see the campfires of her brothers and cousins across the river at night. They talk of messages and visits and the like. You can feel the fear and concern each has for the other.

In addition, part of Miss Haw's article describes her visit to the Watt house two months after the June 27th battle. Her description of the aftermath in terms of what remained, the ghastly sights and smells, and the overall resulting losses to all involved is testimony to the ravages of war.

Miss Haw also describes old traditions and family rituals such as quilting where granddaughters gather to make quilts for Grandmother Watt's sons. Her detailed and loving description of the history and significance of some of the material used in the quilts is priceless. It gives us an insight into what has been lost in our mobility and lack of time for family and the passing of family lore and tradition from generation to generation. Today, we refer to this as oral history.

Even though these articles were written over the period of some thirty years, they confirm and identify many of the same people, events, dates, places. They help to validate and provide some reliability to much of what we know today. All of these articles are valuable assets in piecing together "burned county" history.

After reading all of the articles, one has to remember that they are anecdotal remembrances and recollections. For historical and genealogical purposes, one must rely on primary sources such as court records, military records and Bible records. The articles can serve as starting points. The Hooper and Haw articles are interrelated and cross-referenced with the 1850 Census for Hanover and Henrico Counties and with articles and pictures or sketches of the homes and plantations about many of the subjects. All of this information is included and is a must read.

ENJOY!

PART ONE

THE AUTHORS

About Reverend Tom

Thomas (Tom) Williamson Hooper was the fourth child of Joseph (1807-1852) and Elizabeth Carleton Haw (1806-1879). He married Lettie W. Johnson on 18 January 1860 in Hanover County, Virginia. Tom spent his childhood at Beaver Dam Farm which his father acquired around 1835 from Mrs. William White. At the time of Joseph Hooper 's death in 1852, Tom's mother sold the farm and moved into Richmond City. Piecing events together, Tom was attending school, probably Hampden-Sydney College at this time. The following sketch of his life has been copied from the *Bassett-French Biographical Sketches* in the Library of Virginia in Richmond.

> Hooper, Rev. Thomas W., D. D., Presbyterian Minister, son of Joseph R ., b. in Hanover Co. Nov. 2nd, 1837; grad. H. S. Coll. 1855, taking the first honors of his class, and the Orators Medal of the Union Society; attended Union Sem.. N. Y., four months; returned to Union Theo. Sem.; was licensed to preach by Hanover Presbytery (N. S.) 1857; ordained and installed Pastor of Pole Green Church, Feby 1858; Pastor of Liberty Church, 1863; Pastor of Christiansburg Church, 1865; Pastor 2nd Presbyterian Church, Lynchburg, 1870; removed to Alabama and charge of the Presbyterian Church at Selma, Al. 1876; Trustee of H. S. Coll.; received the title of D. D. from Roanoke Coll. 1876; was for twelve years stated clerk of Montgomery Presbytery also chairman Presbyterian Committee Home Missions; member Executive Committee Colored Theo. Inst., Tuskaloosa [sic], Ala,; chairman, Executive Committee, Orphan's Home, Tuskegee, Ala.; has been a frequent contributor to the religious prose for over thirty years, and orator of sermons, tracts, addresses, etc.

A biographical sketch of Thomas Hooper appeared in the *Confederate Veteran Magazine,* Volume XXIV, page 83:

> Rev. Thomas W. Hooper, D.D., died at the home of his son in Culpeper, Va., on November 26, 1915. He was born in Hanover County, Va., November 2, 1832. He graduated from Hampden-Sidney [sic] College and also from the Union Theological Seminary, in Virginia, and was ordained as a minister of the Presbyterian Church in the following year, 1858. He served as Pastor of different Churches in his native State, his pastorate of the Church at Christiansburg being especially notable in that he served it from 1865 to 1870 and was called back to that Church in 1888 and

continued in its service until his retirement in 1906. Dr. Hooper was greatly beloved and highly honored by all who knew him. An injury to his right hand in infancy prevented Dr. Hooper from serving in the ranks of the Confederate army, but he served as an army chaplain while also serving as a pastor of Liberty Church. He was Chaplain of the U. C. V. Camp at Christiansburg.

His service was documented in The *Southern Historical Society Papers,* Volume 39, page 102:

Union Theological Seminary, Hampden-Sidney [sic], Virginia in the Confederate Army.

Thos. W. Hooper and Moses D. Hogue [sic] are listed as Chaplains. [Note: Moses Drury Hoge was a Chaplain of the Confederate Congress and for the soldiers at Camp Lee in Richmond, Virginia during the Civil War.(Also listed is Hugh Augustus White, Captain, killed at Second Manassas, Aug. 31, 1862.)

Two Faces of Rev. Thomas Williamson Hooper, D. D.

A.B., 1855. First Honor. Union Seminary, 1858; D.D., Roanoke College, 1875. Trustee Hampden-Sydney College, 1872–1913. Presbyterian preacher. Post Chaplin. Liberty, Va., Orator, 1858. ΒΦΠ Convention. Died 1915, Culpeper, Va. The picture is supplied by the son, the Rev. Thomas W. Hooper, ΠΚΑ, Culpeper, Va. (Source: *Zeta at Historic Hampden-Sydney, 1850–1912,* by Karl W. Fisher, p. 515.)

Photo provided by James F. (Foote) Hooper of painting located at the First Presbyterian Church of Selma, AL.

About Joseph Richardson Haw

The following death notice has been taken from the *Confederate Veteran Magazine,*, Volume XXXVII, page 146.

Capt. Joseph Richardson Haw

Adjutant of the R. E. Lee Camp No. 5, of Hampton, Va., and one of the leading Confederates of that section, died at his home in Hampton in January after a brief illness, aged eighty-four years. He was born at Oak Grove in Hanover County, Va., December 14, 1845, the son of John Haw III and Mary Austin Watt both of Virginia ancestry.

Joseph Haw and four brothers fought in the Southern army. He was in the Confederate ordnance department in Richmond; and, during the winter of 1864-65, he served in the trenches in front of Richmond as a member of the 1st Battalion, Local Defense Troops. When Richmond was evacuated, he made his way on foot to the South and joined Company A, 4th Batallion, Tennessee Cavalry, Dibrell's Division of Wheeler's Command, which escorted President Davis to Georgia, and young Haw was with it until its surrender on May 10, 1865.

A member of the second class to graduate from the Virginia Polytechnic Institute at Blacksburg, where he was a cadet lieutenant, instructor, and prize debater, Comrade Haw was also the oldest graduate at the time of his death. He later studied law at the University of Virginia, and then, as a civil engineer, he was employed in the construction of the Northern Pacific Railroad in the Dakotas. He had been a resident of Hampton since 1889, and in charge of the Hampton Foundry for many years. In 1896, he became chief engineer in the quartermaster's department at Fort Monroe, retiring in 1922. He served as adjutant of the R. E. Lee Camp, U. C. V., for more than twenty-eight years, and stood high in the organization, having served on general staffs. He had contributed a number of articles to the *Confederate Veteran Magazine* being one of the best informed in the history of the Confederacy. From early life he was a member of the Presbyterian Church and was one of the leaders in the Church at Hampton, serving as ruling elder for many years.

In 1891, Capt. Haw was married to Miss Mary A. Cumming, of Hampton, who survives him with one son, Maj. Joseph Cumming Haw, of the 61st Coast Artillery; also one brother, George P. Haw.

He was of the old school of Virginia gentlemen, loyal to the South, a true friend, a generous contributor to those in need, a man of the strictest integrity and the highest Christian character.

About Mary Jane Haw

Mary Jane Haw was the author of two known novels and a "Story and Incident: My Visits to Grandmother"published in the the *Christian Observer*, Volume 9, May 18, 1910 [Louisville], pp. 22-23. Also included is the diary entry "Stuley [sic]: The Birthplace of Patrick Henry."

Her first work which turned into the novel *The Rivals, A Chickahominy Story* started as an entry in a contest in which it won $1,000.00 as best illustrated romance (novel/story) and was published in 1864.

In 1889, *The Beechwood Tragedy, A Tale of the Chickahominy* was published.

Miss Haw was born 15 Sep 1835 at "Oak Grove" in Hanover County, Va. to John Haw III (1802 – 1873) and Mary Austin Watt (1805 – 1883). Her father and uncle married sisters.

Mary Jane never married. She died in Portsmouth, Virginia on 26 Mar 1927 and is buried in Hollywood Cemetery in Richmond, Virginia.

There is no known image of Mary Jane Haw.

PART TWO

THE ARTICLES

Rivhmond Dispatch

Richmond, Virginia
Sunday, February 3, 1895

ABOUT "BEAVERDAM"

INTERESTING RECOLLECTIONS OF THE HANOVER VILLAGE

NOTABLE NATIVES OF THE PLACE

The Writer Tells Charming Stories of the School Days of the "Old
Boys"- Thrilling War and
Other Historical Incidents Related

(written for the *Dispatch*)

Thirty years had passed since I had the privilege of visiting the scene of my boyhood. It is now the property of Mr. Catlin, of Richmond, though the residence of a tenant. It stands overlooking the Beaver Dam Creek and Ellerson's mill, and was the main portion of the field over which was fought the first of the series of battles around Richmond [June 26-27, 1862]. A good picture of the house and environs and also of the ruins of the mill hangs on my study wall, cut from the war articles of the *Century* [*Illustrated Monthly Magazine*].

On pious purpose bent, one Sunday in November, I walked in rain and mud around the old homestead, where were passed the pleasant days of a studious but happy boyhood.

My father bought the place from old Mrs. William White, whom I vaguely remember as a resident of her son's home on Church Hill. This was Mr. P. B. [Philip B.] White, of the firm of Massie & White, at the corner of an alley on Main between Fifteenth and Sixteenth. There was a maiden daughter left in those days, Miss Elizabeth White, a boon companion of my mother. "Liz" and "Betsy" they called each other, and when my mother came to Richmond the carriage always called at Mr. Cullingworth's, on Union Hill, and Liz came over to dine and get sick from over-sumptuous fare with Betsy when the shopping hours were over. From those dinners I do not wonder at the size of her son, your worthy postmaster, as he seems to have had a constitution to digest them.

Rev. Dr. William S. [Spotswood] White, pastor of Stonewall Jackson, was also a son of Capt. Billy White[1] and was born at Beaver Dam, and so was Mr. Thomas White, who lived at the house on Mechanicsville turnpike

15

afterwards owned by Rev. Dr. Leonidas Rosser. This Mr. White moved to Missouri, a kind of Western Eldorado, when I was a boy.

At Mechanicsville lived a Mr. [John T.] Chesterman, whose son, Alonzo D., was a schoolmate of mine, and now is an honored professor in the University of Mississippi. He is a cousin, I think, of your facetious "Idle Reporter," who ought to have been born, along with Henry Clay, Patrick Henry, and the rest of us in, or near the "slashes of Hanover." At the "head of the turnpike," now dubbed Mechanicsville, was also a Tappahannock stage stand, kept by Mr. Achiles Lumpkin, the father of Dr. John L., whose name was universally called by the negroes "Mars' Kills Lukins."

Near the village also lived Mr. [William A.] Binford [of Waverly], one of our most progressive farmers, who was the first of our neighbors to introduce Peruvian guano -- pronounced "juano" by the negroes. Across the road from my old home lived Mr. George Washington Truehart[2], with a very large and most respectable family. The old gentleman had a vineyard, and, like Noah, he made some wine, pressing out the juice in my father's cider-press, and storing it to ripen in the cellar. Then he got him a round phial to fit the bung-hole, and tied a string to it, and tasted that wine from day to day until he acquired a thirst for strong drink. Then calamities came on him, and he moved South. The family were members of Dr. Plumer's church, and sometimes on Sunday evening the Doctor would come out and preach to us in the parlor.

ACCOUNTED FOR SIZE

Dr. Plumer never forgot a face or name, and when I met him unexpectedly at my own door in Alabama he remarked, "You are not as large as your father." A few moments afterwards I asked, "Doctor, do you remember that you used to preach at Mr. Truehart's when I was a boy?" "Certainly," he said, "they were members of my church." The doctor was old school and my father was a new school elder, hence he was looking after his sheep. "Well," said I, "I remember that during one of those services some other boys and myself got to cutting up while you were preaching, and you just turned around and walled those big eyes of yours at us, and it scared me out of ten years' growth." With a twinkle of the eye, but with his deep toned voice, he said: "That accounts for your not being as large as your father, I suppose?" Mr. Truehart sold out to Dr. Arson when he moved South, and to show the neighborly feeling of the community, I remember that at the sale of personal effects my father bought an old pair of wheels and axletree of a cart, which had been borrowed from our house and worn out at Mr. Truehart's.

My first school days were passed here, and one of the daughters of the worthy house taught me my letters. But I mistook thunderwood [poison sumac] for elder and became poisoned in the effort to make a popgun, and this cut short my scholastic efforts for several weeks.

EARLY EDUCATION THOROUGH

The principal [sic] school for our neighborhood, however, was Meadow Farm Academy, at the residence of Mr. William B. Sydnor. At that time, I think, Mr. Sydnor had twelve children, and my father about ten in all. Dr. [Henry] Curtis had quite a number, Mr. Miller Macon a large family, and so we had a full school. The daily session opened as soon as we could get there after an early breakfast, and we got home after sundown. And I make bold to say that education in the country in those days, in all its essential elements, was more thorough and lasting, if not as diversified, than it is to-day, with all our modern appliances for "education made easy." And while the patrons who were able to do so were expected to pay tuition fees, no worthy boy or girl was rejected on account of the lack of funds.

I am also such an "Old Fogy" as to insist upon it that we had more real, unadulterated fun in those days than the young people do these days. Our fathers had an unpleasant habit sometimes, if we had laid a scheme for a hunt or a fishing without consulting them, of nipping our nascent plans in the bud by telling us to cut wood, or shell corn, or, in the spring, plant corn. But I had two hounds and the Sydnor boys had several, while our genial neighbor, Captain [William Smith] Austin, would swear that we should not have his; still boys and hounds have an instinctive affinity for each other, and when one of our dogs would hear the yelp of another or the blast of a horn we were obliged to see what the matter was. The now famous historic Chickahominy heard sweet music in those days, when we were after Bre'r Rabbit, or Bre'r 'Possum, or Bre'r Coon. Bre'r Fox was, in those days, "a huckleberry above our persimmon."

Then, too, we played squirrel, climbing trees, and jumping from limb to limb. Instead of the brutal base-ball and foot-ball of today, we had chermany, roly-boly, little cat, bandy, and stung each other with dogwood berries, shot from pop-guns.

SAD CHANGES

But, returning to Beaver Dam, what sad changes have come over these scenes of my childhood! The most of the outhouses are gone, and the ashes of our family circle, once buried there, sleep in Hollywood [Cemetery]. But the old home still stands, hoary with age, and yet precious to memory. The last time I stood under the roof was a few days after the battle, and all around me were the unburied dead, while the house and trees were cut to pieces by cannon and innie-balls.

The editor of the *Century [Illustrated Monthly Magazone]* states in a foot-note to the picture of the house: "The Confederates came across the open hills and down the slope and along the road (offering their flank to the Union artillery) to the line of the creek (shown by the trees below the bridge), but did not cross it. Their loss in the engagement was frightful. Dr. Catlin's son says that the slope of the hill was fairly covered with dead and wounded. The Catlin farm was occupied by Ripley's Brigade of D. H. Hill's Division, and by Pender's Brigade of A. P. Hill's. The Forty-fourth Georgia alone lost 125 in killed and wounded, and its efforts to reform in the rear without officers are described as pathetic. "Good heavens!" said spectators, "is this all of the Forty-fourth Georgia?"

The Battlefield of Beaver Dam Creek at Ellerson's Mill, drawn by Harry Fenn after photograph **by E. S. Anderson** *in Century Illustrated Monthly Magazine* , June 1885 (v. XXX, n. 2, p. 301). Beaver Dam (Hooper House, known as Catlin House during War) located at upper left corner.

MINISTERS OF THE GOSPEL

But while Beaver Dam is historic as a scene of one of our most terrific battles, from under that old roof have gone forth no less than nine ministers of the Gospel. Dr. William S. White has left to the Church Dr. George

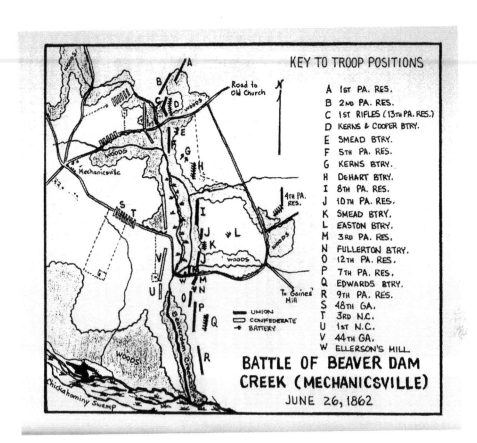

KEY TO TROOP POSITIONS

A 1ST PA. RES.
B 2ND PA. RES.
C 1ST RIFLES (13TH PA. RES.)
D KERNS & COOPER BTRY.
E SMEAD BTRY.
F 5TH PA. RES.
G KERNS BTRY.
H DeHART BTRY.
I 8TH PA. RES.
J 10TH PA. RES.
K SMEAD BTRY.
L EASTON BTRY.
M 3RD PA. RES.
N FULLERTON BTRY.
O 12TH PA. RES.
P 7TH PA. RES.
Q EDWARDS BTRY.
R 9TH PA. RES.
S 48TH GA.
T 3RD N.C.
U 1ST N.C.
V 44TH GA.
W ELLERSON'S MILL

BATTLE OF BEAVER DAM
CREEK (MECHANICSVILLE)
JUNE 26, 1862

Military Operations in Hanover County, 1861-1865, by John M. Gabbert, p. 32.

William White, of Moorfield, W. Va. and Dr. Henry M. White of Winchester.
Dr. George White has a son, Rev. Ashlin White, of Girardstown.

Dr. Henry M. White has two sons — Rev. William McWhite, of
Richmond, and Rev. R. W. White, a missionary to China. Dr. William S.
White had another son who was a seminary student — the gallant Captain
Hugh White — killed at Manassas. Mr. P. B. White has a son, Dr. Thomas
Ward White, now of Texas. And from the same old home, I, too, have come
to preach the same Gospel, which was learned of our parents at Beaver
Dam.

Near Cold Harbor stands the [Garthright] house[3] where my father was
born and not far from the house there is a graveyard, surrounded by a brick
wall, with a half-circle brick along the top. There sleep the generations of
my forefathers. In that enclosure is buried Mr. James Hooper, and at his
funeral Rev. Samuel Darius [Davies] officiated on August 21, 1756 and

preached a most powerful sermon (in his published sermons) on the text selected by the good man before his death, I Peter, iv, 18.

The introduction to the sermon follows. It is taken from *Substance of Sermons by Samuel Davies, A.M., Formerly President of Nassau Hall.*

SAINTS SAVED WITH DIFFICULTY
AND THE CERTAIN PERDITION OF SINNERS

And if the righteous scarcely be saved, where shall the ungodly and the sinner appear?

"This text may sound in your ears like a message from the dead; for it is at the request of our deceased friend that I now insist upon it. He knew so much from the trials he made in life, that if he should be saved at all, it would be with great difficulty, and if he should escape destruction at all, it would be a very narrow escape; and he also knew so much of this stupid, careless world, that they stood in need of a solemn warning on this head; and therefore desired that his death should give occasion to a sermon on this alarming subject. But now the unknown wonders of the invisible world lie open to his eyes; and now he can take a full review of his passage through this mortal life; now he sees the many unsuspected dangers he narrowly escaped, and the many fiery darts of the devil which the shield of faith repelled; now like a ship arrived in port, he reviews the rocks and shoals he passed through, many of which lay under water and out of sight; and therefore now he is more fully acquainted with the difficulty of salvation than ever. And should he now rise and make his appearance in this assembly in the solemn and dread attire of an inhabitant of the world of spirits and again direct me to a more proper subject methinks he would still stand to his choice and propose it to your serious thoughts, that 'If the righteous man is scarcely saved, where will the impious and Sinner appear?' "

AN EPISODE

In the winter of 1860 I was snow-bound for a time at Marion, Smyth county. Soon after my arrival a gentleman, 85 years of age, Mr. Thomas Thurmond, sought an introduction to me, stating that we were distant cousins. At first I was incredulous, but while recent events soon passed away from his memory, the smallest events of fifty or sixty years ago seemed indelible. He said his mother was a Hooper, and was born near Cold Harbor, and that a sister of hers married a Drewery [Drewry], who owned the Falls Plantation, opposite Richmond. He accurately described the house, the cedar lane, and the graveyard enclosed with a brick wall, round on the top, although he had not seen the place for fifty years. He then said, with a peculiar look, "What become of Miss Sally [Sarah Bohannon] Kidd?" Hesitating a moment, I asked, "How old would she be now?" "About 75 years old." "Oh, yes," said I, "she is a member of my church, and we call her old Mrs. Hugh Watt[4] and her son George is my brother-in-law, and two of her daughters married my uncles — John and Richardson Haw."

Lost in thought for a moment, the old man looked up, and with a chuckling laugh, said: "I courted that girl once. I met her at Colonel Atkinson's funeral, and fell in love with her on sight. I managed to go home with her to dinner, and was so dead in love that I courted her. She kicked me, but she kissed me."

As soon as I returned home I made a pastoral visit. I found the old lady as prim and precise as the old Virginia matrons were wont to be. She always called me Thomas, and had a very suggestive prayer she often ejaculated when annoyed, "The Lord give me patience!"

I told her of my trip to Southwest Virginia, and incidentally remarked that I met an old friend of hers, rather an old beau, a Mr. Thomas Thurmond. "The Lord give me patience!" instantly exclaimed the dear old lady, with a blush to the roots of her gray hair. "Yes," she said, "I remember meeting him at Colonel Atkinson's funeral." And, said I, "got your father to invite him home to dinner." "No such thing, sir; he managed to get an invitation and came." "Yes," said I, "and courted you!" "What if he did?" with a quick flash, and without a prayer. "Oh, nothing in the world," said I, "but there is a mystery about it. He says you promptly discarded him, but that you kissed him. I want you to explain that." With all the honest indignation of a virtuous maidenhood flashing back over fifty years she said: "Well, he told you a lie, sir; he asked me to kiss him, but I declined. The Lord give me patience!" I honestly believe she did. But "one touch of nature makes all the world akin."

> "Visions of childhood, stay, O stay!
>   Ye are so sweet and wild;
>   A voice from out of the future cries —
>   Away! Away! You are no more a child."
>   T. W. H.

Article Notes

1.   Captain William White [(30 Jul 1773-10 Sep 1820), m. Mildred Ellis (3 Jan 1777-22 Jan 1845) issue: Phillip B., Elizabeth, William S. (30 Jul 1800-29 Nov 1873), m. Jane Isabella Watt (18 Oct 1803-6 Oct 1878), Thomas J., Harriet E., and Elizabeth].

2.   George Washington Truehart m. Fanny G. Overton, bond 7 Jan 1801.

3.   The house near Cold Harbor where T. W. Hooper's father was born is probably the Garthright House. This conclusion is drawn from the description of the cemetery wall in this article and the owner during the Civil War being Miles Garthright whose wife was Joseph Hooper's sister. This in essence shows the property still in the Hooper family.

4.   Hugh Watt m. Sarah (Sally) Bohannon Kidd, (17 Apr 1802). She was the daughter of Pitman Kidd of Essex, later Hanover County, Virginia.

Richmond Dispatch

Richmond, Virginia
Sunday, February 10, 1895

THOSE GOOD OLD DAYS

MORE REMINISCENCES OF EARLY LIFE AT BEAVER DAM

How He Outwitted His Father and Tasted of Forbidden Fruit
Preaching to the Negroes

(written for the Dispatch)

Your kind comments on a former article, touching the scenes of Beaver Dam, my boyhood home, have embolded me to write out a few more reminiscences. Those good old days are gone, and since Dr. Bagby died and T. N. [Thomas Nelson] Page got married and Uncle Remus went back on "the little boy" there are only a few, now and then, to keep fresh flowers on the grave where so many southern hopes and memories lie buried. Slavery in Virginia meant easy times for the negroes and hard work for the master and mistress. Had my father not had other employments he would have been compelled to sell a negro now and then to keep both whites and blacks from starving. The farm, from which were sold some hay, some wheat, some fruit, including watermelons, never did pay expenses. The negroes were well fed and clothed, and when sick had the best medical attention, and were carefully nursed by mother and "Aunt" Nancy.

AUNT NANCY

She was fat and dumpy, and smoked a corn-cob pipe with a reed stem three inches long, saturated with nicotine, until it was as black as her ebony complexion. But strong as that pipe and tobacco were, when I was going to the barn about daybreak to give out corn for the horses, and she to milk the cows, I would get her to wipe the stem with her apron and put it in my own mouth, and smoke. "Stolen waters are sweet," and it may be that this was a factor in the case, but those quiet whiffs of smoke from "Aunt" Nancy's pipe were sweeter to me on a frosty morning that the best Havana has tasted since. She had an unhallowed way of saying, "My God!" and, boy as I was, I rebuked her for it, when she turned to me and said: "La, Mars' Tom, who is I got to call on but my Laurd." I was silenced, but not convinced. One night I was near her comfortable log-house when I heard a

23

cat, on a regular serenade, and then I heard the old women sing out "God, cat almos' talk! Scat!" and I was glad of it, for I was scared myself.

MISCHIEVOUS PRANKS

The younger negroes were our playmates. I had an older brother [Joseph R. Hooper, 1829-1845] living then, and many a time he and Burrel, a negro boy, got me into pretty bad scrapes. My father had every kind of apple, cherry, peach, pear, quince, and berry that were common in those days. One autumn he packed up a hogshead of winesap apples, in sand, in the corner of the log cornhouse. We boys, white and black, hankered after those apples many a day, but could not reach them. At last, Brother Joe found an iron rod with a sharp end, and, climbing up on the logs, he would insert it between the logs, stick up an apple, and then carefully swing it around and hand it to us. We were just having a regular pic-nic when father walked around the corner, switch in hand, and as he lit into the older boys, I lit out for the house and my mother's protecting arms.

When John B. Gough [temperance orator] came around my father signed the pledge so honestly and fervently for the whole family that he resolved to cut us off, even from sweet cider. He had a lot of hogsheads placed on two parallel logs, and in these he put the pomace, or ground apples, intending them to get as sour as vinegar before he pressed out the juice. I seem to have inherited an inventive genius from him, and as we regarded it a fair fight between father and sons I determined to get at that cider before it turned too sour to drink. Securing a half-gallon vegetable gourd, with a short handle, used in those days, I got on my back between the logs and squirmed my way until I got to the bung in the end of the hogshead. It was driven in tight, but I came out and got a brickbat and went back again. I loosened the plug and then pulled — yes, pulled — and the plug came out before I looked for it, and never was a boy so saturated with lengthened sweetness long drawn out. I got my gourd full, but before I could get that plug back in the bung I was saturated from head to foot, and I supposed I must have smelled of whipped cider for a week.

GHOSTS

I got myself into another scrape when I was large enough to handle a gun. Down on the farm near the Chickahominy is Sugar-Loaf Island, which was reputed to be the place where John Smith was captured. To a boy taught by negroes to believe in ghosts, the truth of history has but little weight. I had heard the tradition, and the beech trees on that curious mound were filled with names and hieroglyphics carved on the bark. I was sitting there late one evening, all alone, watching for a squirrel, gun in hand. The silence of twilight came on, and I began to think of Captain

John Smith and the Indians, and wondered how a fellow would feel if some of the redskins came bounding out, with tomahawk and scalping-knife, and before I knew it, as the boys say, "I got a move on me." Before I had gotten quite out of breath, I remembered that I had to pass the negro graveyard, and by the time I had safely passed that, I recalled the fact that the family burying-ground was also in my way. When I got home, pale and breathless, I was very glad, but I never would tell what made me so nervous and scared that night.

THE DOCTOR OUTWITTED

At last, school-days were over, and I went off to college. I had been there about a session and a half, when I was taken home on a bed by my kind and devoted father. For months, my life seemed to hang on a thread, but at last I began slowly to come back from the very borders of the grave. The treatment of this dread disease — typhoid fever — in those days was very different from what it is now. Parched and blistered on tongue and lips with thirst, not a piece of ice nor a drop of water was allowed to cool and refresh. Flaxseed tea in a yellow pitcher with blue flowers still sits there by the fireplace, and the wild and weird dreams of delirious hunts for cool spring and apples hidden in the strawstacks haunt me to this day. Even when I was strong enough to be lifted into a rocking-chair, and was hungry enough to breed a famine on the farm and to eat all the good things sent in by our kindly neighbors, I was limited to three slices of bakers bread toasted and three cups of hot-water tea per day.

In thinking of that spell of sickness I have often thought of the old gentleman in Greenbrier county [now West Virginia] who was riding through the woods in a terrific wind. At last a large, forked whiteoak came crashing down — one fork before him and the other behind — killing the horse, but not hurting the man. In describing the scene he always said: "Ah! It was one of the Lord's mercies, and a thousand pities that I was not killed."

But I outwitted the kind old doctor and took matters in my own hands. I was well enough to be helped down the steps to the level of the yard, and walk alone in the early springtime. Dismissing my nurse I strolled about for awhile, and when the coast was clear I made for the kitchen. "Aunt" Lucy was "mighty glad and proud to see me in my old seat by the big, open fireplace, where I had eaten a second breakfast with her on fatty-bread and coffee every Sunday morning when a boy." But I knew my furlough from my dear old mother would be short, so I said at once, "Aunt'" Lucy, bake me an ashcake and broil me one of those herrings strung on that stick just as soon as you can." "Lawd, Mars' Tom, dey'll kill you sure." "Never you mind, if you love me give me something to eat, for I am starving to death by inches." She soon had them ready, and I ate the whole ashcake and the whole herring. Then I washed my hands and mouth, strolled around, feeling, as Uncle Remus would say, "mighty biggoty." Then I was helped up the steps and took my accustomed chair.

My mother asked me where I had been, and I told her I had strolled around the yard; and as I never could and never did tell a lie, I quietly remarked that I had also gone to the kitchen to see "Aunt" Lucy. I can see her now, sitting in the corner of the fireplace, with her white frilled cap and gold spectacles, knitting away. But as soon as I said kitchen and Aunt Lucy she looked as if struck by electricity and said; "Tom, you've been eating something." "Yes," said I. "I rather think I have." "What is it?" said she. "Mother," I said very deliberately, "I have eaten a whole ashcake and a whole herring." "Well," she said, "you'll be dead before night." Dropping the knitting she bounded out and started all the negroes she could reach after the doctors of the neighborhood.

In half an hour good Dr. [John N.] Ellerson came rushing in, sat down by me, put his hand on my pulse, and looked up with a smile as he said, "Why, his pulse is strong and regular as I ever felt." "Yes," said I, "and you were all starving me to death, and I made up my mind that if I was to die I would die with a full stomach, and not from starvation." But I can still say "It is of the Lord's mercies, and a thousand pities that I was not killed" by that murderous practice.

PREACHING TO THE NEGROES

In 1858, I was called to the (Polegreen) church of my fathers, and accepted. The older people rather demurred, but the younger members took the bit in their mouths and called me, with the assent of the older. No pilgrim ever came to the shrine of most sacred things with more delight and enthusiasm, nor was more cordially received by young and old, white and black. The aged elders had a hard time learning to call me Mister, and the younger people never tried.

Dr. [William F.] Gaines, owner of the famous mill, [Gaines' Mill] became a second father to me, and I shall never forget him nor cease to recall all his deeds of kindness and love. The Doctor and his whole family were received into the church at the same time, and from that day his was a model Christian family. He had a large number of negroes, and for these he felt as Abraham felt toward the slaves of his own patriarchal house. Every Sunday morning the head man blew his horn and the whole set, big and little, had to present themselves, or an excuse for absence, at the school-house. Then the Doctor read the Bible and expounded it while his wife and daughters taught them the "true wisdom."

The prayers of the negroes were always unique, and the Rev. John Jasper never got wilder on science than some of these did in their talks with the Lord. One of the old women, who lived in a cabin by herself, often repeated to me the most wonderful talks she had with the Lord — He coming down the chimney and she sitting before the fire.

But their prayers for me were often ambiguous and embarrassing. They always prayed for me as "their poor little preacher," in what particular sense I never could tell.

The Sunday night after I was married, my bride was overwhelmed with confusion when one of them prayed "that we might be like two doves a-settin' on the same ness'." At another time one of them told me "he had ruther hear me preach than any white man he ever heard, 'cause I preached more like a cullud pusson."

AN HONEST SHEPHERD

I held several funeral services with "Brother Jim," and had the exquisite pleasure of grasping his honest hand a few years since. My cousin told me he had a church of 250 members, and all the white people respected him. He said "Brother Jim" was holding a revival, and there seemed to be a good deal of interest. But one night two sheep "came up missing," and they were traced to some of his members. That night "Brother Jim" said: "Brethren, this meetin' stops tonight. I hear that two sheep done been stole by some of our members. The good Lord don't work when folks is stealin' sheep, and dis meetin' stops right here," and it did.

T. W. H.

Article Notes

T. W. Hooper's older brother was Joseph R. (3 Nov 1829-30 Jan 1845).

Dr. Ellerson, in addition to being a physician, owned Ellerson's Mill prior to it being destroyed during the Civil War.

From the diary of Thomas Garland Tinsley (1788-1859) of Totomoi, Hanover County, VA."Sunday, March 14, 1858: "Seaton (Tinsley, son of T.G. Tinsley), Alex (Tinsley, son of T.G. Tinsley) and Miss Lucy Taliaferro came this morning by cars (railroad from Richmond). Sent my carriage to Water Station (stop on the VA Central Railroad) for them. All went to Church. Mr. Hooper was installed. Mr. Leavenworth preached and Communion in evening. Carried eatables with us. A large congregation. The house full in every part. Mrs. Tinsley, James & self gave $2 for contingent expenses of the Church." (Source: Maria W. Rippe)

Thomas Williamson Hooper m. Lettie W. Johnson on 18 Jan 1860.

Richmond Dispatch

Richmond, Virginia
Sunday, March 3, 1895

POLE GREEN CHURCH[1]

INTERESTING RECOLLECTIONS OF ITS FORMER PLACE

Distinguished Hanoverians Who Were Educated
at Hampden-Sidney [sic]
How to Make an Electrical Machine
Boys Who Had Fun

(written for the *Dispatch*)

In recalling my boyhood days and ministerial days in Hanover, this old church is an object of venerable and pre-eminent importance. Where the name Pole Green came from or what it means no man knoweth to the present day. It was located near the Totpotomoy creek and this name seems to be an Indian version of the Greek. When I first knew it the pulpit looked like an inverted wine-glass, with winding stairs and two closed doors. Near the pulpit was a Precentor's stand, where the "Clarke" stood with his tuning-fork in hand and raised the tunes. There were also square pews for the families of the elders, which were closed, and thus furnished an admirable place for us small children to sleep, under the profound and prolonged services of the day. Over the pulpit was a sounding-board, and back of it a panel, on which some profane finger, dipped in ink, had traced "S. D., 1753." This meant Samuel Davies, the first pastor of the church, and the founder of Presbyterianism in Virginia. The church was modernized in my boyhood, received a cannon-ball from Jackson's flanking army, and was burned in the Grant campaign of 1864 [June 1, from a Confederate artillery shell fired by Sgt. William Spotswood "Buck" White of Beaver Dam Farm

---

1   The Polegreen Church site is now on the National Historic Landmarks Register and the Virginia Register of Historic Places. The site is owned by the Historic Polegreen Church Foundation and is being further developed as a historic site through the efforts of Dr. Robert Bluford and the Foundation. Today's Pole Green probably evolved from the surname Polegreen. George Polegreen had fairly extensive land holdings in the area of Polegreen Corner. The *Vestry Book of Saint Paul's Parish* in 1695 refers to "Polegreen's Quarter, of Beaver Dam Swamp" with further references to "Pole greens Old Field" in 1712, "Polegreen's Old Field in 1717," and to "To begin on Tottopottomy's [sic] Creek, against Polegreen's Old Field." in 1724. Volume 41 of the *Hanover County Historical Society's Bulletin* refers to the Polegreen settlement one mile north of the intersection of Routes 627 (Pole Green Road) & 643 (Rural Point Road).

Historic Polegreen Church. Pamunkey Woman's Club Calendar, January, 1996 by Bettie Broyles Cole.

while trying to dislodge Union sharpshooters, and the same day Beulah Church was burned].

MY PREDECESSORS

Josh Billings says, "When I hear a man bragging about his ancestors I always feel sorry -- for his ancestors." This curt sarcasm is as applicable to preachers as to other people, but when the best part of our ancestors are under the ground we ought not to forget them.

Parson [John D.] Blair one of *The Two Old Parsons* by George Wythe Munford, 1884], a book that ought to be read by every one who has read *The Innocents Abroad*, was pastor of Pole Green, alternating with his church in Richmond. And without any disrespect to your city people, he showed his practical good sense by choosing for his wife a Hanover girl, a Miss [Mary] Winston, daughter of Major [Geddes] Winston, in whose lane I have gathered chinquapins when I was a boy.

I need not say that this was before my day. The first pastor of whom I have a distinct recollection was Parson Henry Smith, who graduated at Hampden-Sidney [sic] and Union Seminary. He was very tall, very thin, very solemn, and never knew how to preach to children or negroes. He rode around in a "sulky," and when that was at the gate we boys avoided the parlor until we were summoned to family prayers. But he was a good man, and in after years I found him most genial and agreeable, and when I was far from home he treated me as a son. My uncle John Haw, who had more dry humor than any man I ever saw, used to say that Parson Smith ought to sing well, because he had feet like a mocking-bird -- the leg striking the foot about half way, leaving the heel about as long as the rest of the foot.

But the only pastor I ever appreciated was the late Dr. Henry S. Osborn. He was in Palestine while I was so near death with typhoid-fever, and his aged father filled his place during his absence. The old gentleman died at the residence of the elder General St. George Cocke, near Bremo Bluff, and is buried there.

Mr. Osborn was the exact opposite of Parson Smith, and his coming was hailed by everybody, young and old, with the greatest delight. He preached in a sprightly, lively way, and sometimes not more than fifteen minutes. He rode around from house to house, hearing us recite the "Shorter Catechism" -- the hardest book to memorize and the hardest to forget I ever studied. He always carried with him chemicals and little instruments for experiments, and thus awakened in us a thirst for knowledge which led to college education in after days.

COLLEGE STUDENTS

In compiling the alumni catalogue of Hampden-Sidney [sic], I was surprised at the number of students who had gone there from old Hanover. Among the first were Dr. William S. White and his cousin, Mr. William B. Sydnor. Then came a Mr. Roane, two Sheltons, who moved to Mississippi; and one of these sent a son who is now an eminent lawyer in Vicksburg Captain S. M. Shelton; the late Dr. John L. Shepperson, and his brother, Dr. C. M. Shepperson, now of Hampden-Sidney [sic], were born in Hanover, near the New Kent line; Dr. Leo William Pollard, still living, in extreme old age, and his son, the gallant Bernard Pollard, supposed to have been killed in a cavalry charge at Spotsylvania Courthouse, Dr. Thomas Pollard:; Messrs. James B. and Reuben E. Gardner; Dr. Alek Tinsley (then to William & Mary and medical school in New York), and his brothers, Seaton G. [actually studied at William & Mary] and James G. Tinsley, of Richmond; Professor Alonzo D. Chesterman, and the two sons of Captain Meredith, of Hanover. All of these were educated at old Hampden-Sidney [sic], and we younger men owe our aspirations for a college education largely to the

31

inspiration of our pastor, Dr. H. S. [Henry] Osborn, as some of the older men owed theirs to Dr. John H. Rice.

PRACTICAL EXPERIMENT

Mr. Osborn taught me how to make an electrical machine. My mother gave me a glass preserve-jar, holding a gallon. He taught me how to mix Spanish-brown[2] and beeswax, to cement wood and glass, and to use amalgam from broken mirrors and lard for a rubber. A kind china merchant on Main street looked amused and then interested when I asked for some pieces of broken looking-glasses. But when I told him my object he went right to work and loaded me down, as good men always will do with anybody who means business. My father had a turning lathe near the mill, run by water from the ice-pond, and there I spent a good deal of my spare time. Rather than let me break his turning-chisels, Mr. Joe Grubbs turned the uprights and spindles, etc., for me, and I put it together. As the boys say now, "She was a daisy." I could shock a circle of fifteen or twenty and send them screaming away.

That same Uncle John Haw was at our house, and, being an inventive genius, he saw my machine, and I knew I had him. "What's that, Tom?" I explained it and told him how I could shock him. He said he didn't believe a word of it. I loaded her for bear. He put his hand on the Leyden jar and slowly held his knuckle to the ball. I don't think he cursed, but he used a word that is often combined with the name of God, and knocked my Leyden jar about ten feet off the table. I could never get him to monkey with that buzz-saw again.

P.S. -- Among other kind words touching my first article on Beaver Dam, I have a very pleasant letter from my old school-mate, whom I have not seen for many years, Walter Sydnor, Esq., of your city. He says: "The next time you feel reminiscent and philosophical please explain why it is that boys of this day do not have as much pure and unadulterated fun as the ante-bellum boys had. That such is a fact is in my opinion certainly true." I answer there are two reasons.

1. We played for fun. Base-ball and foot-ball, as now played, are directly, or indirectly, for money -- either as bets or as expenses paid.

2. In our day every boy had his part in the fun. Take charmeny. Two of the best players were appointed captains. These alternately selected the next best, until the sides were nearly equally divided, and the smallest "kid" in school was a man on one side or the other. Now a "battery" of two, with the help of seven outsiders, do the work, while the rest stand around and yell like a tribe of Comanche Indians. This "battery" is almost always

---

2   Spanish-brown earth has a dark reddish brown color because of the presence of iron oxide and used as a pigment — also known as *Indian Red.*

composed of professionals, even in college "mines" or misnamed students, who study base-ball instead of college text books.

When the Shah of Persia was in London he expressed his amusement at the noble and cultured ladies and gentlemen wearying themselves with dancing. He said in his country he hired all that hard work for his amusement. So it is now, with the order reversed. We "old boys" used to make and have our own fun. In these degenerate days the dudes pay the players, so-called, with the gate receipts, and look on and holler and bet.

T. W. H.

Richmond Dispatch

Richmond, Virginia
Sunday, March 10, 1895

HANOVER MEMORIES

HOW DEAR TO THE HEART ARE THE SCENES OF OUR CHILDHOOD

Recollections of Incidents When Going to
School at Laurel Meadow.
Education in Past Compared with that of the Present

(written for the *Dispatch*)

My first article in the *Dispatch* on Beaver Dam has brought me many letters from old schoolmates whom I have not seen for forty years. They came from different states, showing how widely the *Dispatch* is read, and "how dear to the heart are the scenes of our childhood."

From the letter of Mr. Joseph Sydnor, of Columbus, O., I make some extracts of both general and personal interest: "With one or two exceptions, I have a very vivid recollection of every incident mentioned, and went over the ground in my imagination, as I have often done, and enjoyed the scenes again. My impression is that we attended school at Laurel Meadow, or spring (Mr. Truehart's) for a portion of two years -- 1839 and 1840 -- and that a school was opened at Meadow Farm in 1841. How we enjoyed coasting down the hillsides, over the pine tags, whilst seated on a four-inch shingle; wearing away two inches of pants on each side, that our dear old mother had to mend, and who did not neglect to impress on me the importance of being more considerate of her comfort whilst seeking my own pleasure! The "Queen-of-May" celebration that we observed, the flowers for which the larger boys, your brother, and myself, with others, obtained from the genial old bachelor, Mr. Dick Johnson."

"I am quite sure that Dr. Plumer of hallowed memory, held services on Thursday afternoon, once a month, during one summer in the parlor at Laurel Meadow, and later at Beaver Dam. A professor of music, from

Richmond, named Root, undertook to conduct a singing-class here also; but this was for the grown folks."

PRESIDENT JOHN TYLER

"Distinctly do I remember, whilst we were just organizing for a game of little cat, before school called in at Meadow Farm, during the first week in April, 1841, that the Curtis boys came up and announced that President Harrison had just died, and that their uncle, the Vice-President, had been summoned to Washington to succeed as President. Mr. Tyler was on a visit to his brother, Dr. Tyler, at Shermer, in Charles City. The messenger probably stopped at Dr. Curtis's, not knowing whether he would find the Vice-President there or at Dr. Tyler's. Mrs. Curtis was Mr. Tyler's sister. Mr. M. L. Bichford who conducted the school for four years, was quite elated when Bartlet Curtis secured an entrance to West Point from his school.

"I must not close this without bestowing my profound reverence on the memory of the beloved saints, who were held in such high estimate by my dear father. Dr. Plumer, though apparently an austere man, I revered and esteemed highly, and often attended his services after I went to Richmond to business. Your own devoted father was again and again referred to by my father, as a godly man, worthy of all admiration. When sad afflictions came to your house, my own dear parents held him up before us as a model of Christian trust and meekness. Oh, what an inheritance has been left to us -- the memory and examples of such men!"

DR. PLUMER

"Apparently an austere man," says my old school-mate, and he was. But under all that austerity there was a warm heart, and a keen sense of the ludicrous, which Dr. Tucker Lacy could tickle, even at the expense of his very dear friend. Dr. Plumer once said to a friend of mine that the river they were crossing was large enough, and dignified enough, to be called "Thomashigher," instead of being nicknamed "Tom higher." At another time, when a seminary student, at Columbia, preached a sermon from a text, the Doctor's comment was, "If the text had been afflicted with a case of confluent small-pox, the sermon would never have caught it." Messrs. Macfarland and Lyons, too, found that Dr. Plumer had read Don Quixote, and knew how to apply it, to the cost of the lawyers, with a ready wit, as keen and cutting as a Damascus blade. One of the most touching and pathetic scenes I ever read of, was at the close of the funeral services of Mrs. Plumer, in the First Presbyterian church, of your city. Dr. Plumer sent up to the pulpit a request that Dr. Preston, the pastor, should read to the congregation Ruth 1:8: "The Lord deal kindly with you, as ye have dealt with the dead, and with me."

COUNTRY SCHOOL DAYS

When I contrast Meadow Farm Academy with the country schools of the present day, with all due respect to Parson Massey, I consider the latter an unmitigated humbug. The school system now foisted on us, as a Yankee enterprise, suits the thickly-settled districts of the North, and the cities and villages of the South; but it cannot be, or has not been adapted to the sparsely-settled districts, even of our own State. Four months and a half or five months out of twelve for a teacher to pump in, and seven or seven and a half months out of twelve for the contents to pour out of the sifter of a child's thoughtless brain! This always reminds me of our old school-day quiz -- If a frog at the bottom of a well jumps up one foot, and falls back two feet, how long will it take him to get to the top? This, added to another patent fact, public pap is a public curse, shows the folly of the impracticable scheme. It is only in rare cases that the patrons of a public school will prolong the session more than one or two months, if at all, after the free session closes. The result is, that all over our State, and all over the South, the children in the country districts are growing up without even a rudimentary education. And to perpetuate the evil, some of our endowed "State institutions" are compelled to receive these pupils, with scarcely a smattering of English; and in due time send them forth as graduates of certain schools.

NOT SO THEN

With all the odium attached to the phrase, by Young America, I am proud to say, "It was not so when I was a boy."

At Meadow Farm Academy I have just written that Bartlet Curtis was prepared for West Point. There one of the Misses Macon was prepared to adorn and grace the home of her husband, the late Rev. Dr. Alexander Martin, for twenty-five years pastor in Danville, Va. The Sydnor girls were educated for the homes they now grace with refined culture. There I was prepared, with one year's instruction from Dr. Osborn, my pastor, to enter the sophomore class at Hampden-Sidney [sic] College. Latin and Greek were taught, as well as some of the rudiments of science; and all this in a mixed school of girls and boys, by one teacher. But we were in school nearly all day, where we not only recited as now, but studied under the eye and help of the teacher, and not of our parents. I think the vacation was only one month, certainly not more than two. The teacher was well paid a fixed salary, made up by the patrons who could pay, and all who could not pay were admitted free. There were no such trumpery as trustees, but

Mr. William B. Sydnor was boss of the whole affair, appointing the teacher, collecting and paying his salary, and the teacher did the rest in the way of instruction and thrashing combined. We had to "speak," as then called, not declaim, every Friday evening. There, I won my first prize in speaking -- a bright silver half dollar -- over the larger boys. It was a "reward of merit," no doubt, but based on the fact, I expect, of my being the smallest contestant, and the eternal fitness of speech and speaker, the speech being "You'd scarce expect one of my age," etc.

ANOTHER EXPERIMENT

I have told of my electrical machine, of which I was very proud. One of my school chums was Ned Sydnor, who died the night my father did, and within half an hour. I was spending the night with Ned, and early the next morning we found a very heavy frost. I remarked that on such a morning as that if you were to touch the tip of your tongue to a piece of cold iron it would stick. He emphatically denied it, and said I was always fooling around about such fancies. The result was we dressed hurriedly and went out to test the experiment. We found a plow lying in a furrow, with the mould-board white as frost could make it. I urged him not to try it, told him it was according to science, but he laughed at it as bosh and all that. Then he got down on his knees, licked out his tongue, and touched the iron. It caught him like a vice and scared him so that he caught hold of the unstuck part with both hands and pulled, tearing about an inch and a half of skin. He went howling to the house and I "Hit out," as the negroes say, for home, and my breakfast there. Ned told me afterwards that when his mother found out, in spite of his yells, what the matter was, she poured "No. 6" on it, and he thought he was on fire. I didn't see Mrs. Sydnor for some time, or at least she did not see me.

T.W.H.

Article Notes

John Tyler was president from 4 Apr 1841 until 3 March 1845. He had been elected on the Whig ticket as Vice President with William Henry Harrison who died one month into his term. Upon Harrison's death, John Tyler succeeded him and served as the tenth president. He was born in nearby Charles City County. His home there was Sherwood Forest Plantation.

Joseph Hooper died 18 Jun 1852 in Hanover County, Virginia.

Richmond Dispatch

Richmond, Virginia
Sunday, March 31, 1895

OLD TIME POLITICS

A CHAPTER ABOUT THE HENRY-CLAY-
JOHN-MINOR-BOTTS DAYS IN HANOVER

VIVA VOCE FREEHOLD VOTERS

A Typical Politician of Hanover Who Rejoiced in His
Birthplace -- Henry A. Wise and the Know-Nothing Campaign

(written for the *Dispatch*)

The genial Rev. Dr. Sutor, now of Alexandria, once of Liberty, used to
tell how he was caught by a local way, who said to him: "Mr. S., when I
jines the church, I'm goin' to jine yours, because it don't concern itself about
neither politics nor religion." As a general thing, I do not concern myself
about politics, except to vote for the regular nominees of the party, which
in the South ought to have one prominent basis -- vis.: "Self-preservation is
the first law of nature." As Macauley used to say, "the judicious reader" can
form a judgment as to what party I mean.

My father was an old-line, Henry-Clay, John-Minor-Botts Whig, and I
think the most of his neighbors voted the same way. But as I grew up in the
same party, and have continued a Whig to the present day, I may honestly
say that when a boy we, as mother predicted, generally were defeated. The
voting-place was Cold Harbor, and as my father generally took me there on
election-days, as he did to the court-house on the grand day of the "general
muster," I still have a vivid recollection of ginger-cakes, 'simmon-beer,
and cider, on which I feasted, and the drunken brawls that sprang up like
dragons' teeth, from something stronger, among the men.

THREE STIMULANTS

My father was a man of giant strength, amiable word, pleasant
demeanor, and fervent piety. When an old boyhood friend of his, the late
Nathaniel Talley, of Danville, found I was his son, he said with a tear in his
eye and a tremor of the voice: "Well, sir, if you are half as good a man as
your father was you will do." There were only three things that ever excited
him. These were card-playing, religion, and politics. He found some of
his own negroes one night playing cards by moonlight in the kitchen yard,

and told them if he ever found a pack of cards on that place again he would whip the whole farm. I suppose I must have inherited that same horror of the game. Professor Charles H. Winston, that cultivated scholar and noble Christian professor of Richmond College, was my room-mate at Hampden-Sidney [sic] for several years. During one session, when we boarded in a private house at the old courthouse, (now called Worsham), we had two other room-mates. Charles and I would each sit and study at an end of the table, while these "lewd fellows of the baser sort," played "bluff" across the table. One night I was surprised to hear Charles say, as if unconsciously, "Oh, why didn't you play that other card?" This resulted in numerous and noisy invitations to take a hand, and this in a scuffle, which generally ended in his throwing one pack after another into the fire. I need not say that these two students graduated before the end of the session, not on a literary course, but on "Hoyle," and went home.

Religion was the deepest and profoundest subject that could stir up all the depths of my father's nature. When Mr. Osborn, our pastor, went to the Holy Land, he left with each of his elders a book, like *Morning by Morning*, by Spurgeon; and thus, the pastor and each of these read the same words and prayed for each other every day when separated far and wide. It was while he was praying, too, that Dr. William F. Gaines made a profession of religion.

But politics always excited him, a few days before, and especially on the day of election. He would send out his wagon for voters and arrive early at Cold Harbor to work with the non-committals, and still get defeated nearly every time. The *viva voce* voting advocated by Judge Robert Hughes, prevailed in those days, but it was based on landed estate. Nobody could vote unless he owned a small tract of land. A man who owned a house in Richmond would vote on that as a citizen of Richmond; go to Henrico Courthouse and vote again on a few acres of land owned in that county, and then come on out to Cold Harbor and vote again, on a few acres he owned in Hanover. I would be disfranchised if such were the law now, but I would gladly give up my vote if we could get back to those good old days, when a man, though dressed like the Georgia Major, if he owned five acres of land, too poor to sprout black-eyed peas, stood up, and called the name of the man he voted for, and received the gentlemanly bow and thanks of the candidate.

I think it was Talleyrand who said: "Revolutions never go backward. The best way is to join them, and then control them." It is as easy to join them as it was for Mr. Clay to catch that billy-goat by the horns. But how to control them or how to get away from them is about as hard as it was for Mr. Clay to get loose from that goat.

A POLITICIAN OF THAT DAY

I will not call his name, but at my request a friend has given this version of some of his political adventures. He lived at Clay Spring. Politics and Botts so took possession of him that he left his family to take care of themselves, and went about with Botts from place to place when the latter was canvassing for Congress. The people assembled on a court-green to hear Botts would see this busy person arranging the congressman's papers, water, etc., on the table of the platform and making himself generally useful and official. When Mr. Botts had closed his speech he would imagine that people by this time had become intensely anxious to know who he was; and, taking the stand, would gratify their curiosity in the following words:

"Fellow-Citizens, -- I am a gentleman by birth, a scholar by education, a lawyer by profession. I rejoice to say I live at the birthplace of the illustrious Clay, and in the immediate vicinity of the immortal Botts."

A WHIG BARBECUE

It must have been when the "illustrious Clay" was defeated for the presidency I had gone to Richmond with "Goode," one of my father's negro men, who drove a cart loaded with watermelons. He could beat any one crying watermelons I ever heard, especially after he had sold enough to buy him enough whiskey to get about half drunk. This had been accomplished, and we were going down Main street towards Rocketts, when one wheel of the cart dropped into a hole, and broke down. As I had gotten pretty tired of the fun and the keenness of his wit was exhausted I left him, and walked back to Howard's Grove. There were the "log cabin and hard cider," "that same old coon," and all sorts of music; barbecued meats, singing of campaign songs, and some of the grandest speaking I ever heard. But, for all that, the "illustrious Clay," for whom my father had an unbounded admiration, was defeated, and after that he lost much of his zeal for politics, and, like Napoleon after Waterloo, retired to St. Helena.

GOVERNOR HENRY A. WISE

The first vote I ever cast was at Prince Edward Courthouse, while I was a college student. It was in the "Know-Nothing" campaign, the most appropriate name for a political party I ever knew, as agnosticism is in the religious realm. I was initiated by "Blucher Dick Watkins" in the room of a

41

Democratic seminary student, secured in some way for the occasion – "For ways that are dark," etc.

I heard the magnificent speech of Mr. Wise, and admired it as one of the grandest displays of impassioned eloquence I ever heard. But all the same I voted for Colonel Thomas S. Flournoy. The Governor spent one summer at the Rockbridge Baths, the most delightful summer resort at the time I ever attended. My old classmate, the Rev. Dr. Thomas T. Jones and I took a horseback ride that summer over the mountains. At Lexington our old friend, Dr. William S. White advised us to go to the Baths, and we went. When Sunday came, and there was no preacher present, I expect Tom told them that I was a seminary student, and he knew I had one sermon in my saddle-bags, for he had heard it the Sunday before at the Montgomery White. There both of us had sweethearts that summer -- our dear old wives, a thousand times dearer to-day.

I preached, or held forth, to the best of my ability, and after the service the Governor, who was always kind to young men, came forward, took my hand cordially, and made some very pleasant remarks, and introduced me to his son, Henry A. Wise, Jr., who was also, like myself, an "entered apprentice" for the ministry. At that time the Governor could use language that smoked of the kit, and when, by his courtesy, the next day, my friend, "Tem Tit" and I were bathing with him, a small boy tried in vain to get in, and at last climbed to the top of the partition. He must have thought that a hurricane, from a place hotter than the torrid regions, had struck up and swept him clear out of the bathing-house.

THE EASTERN SHORE

Soon after I settled in Hanover, as pastor of Pole Green, I went to the Eastern Shore to help ordain and install a pastor at Accomac Courthouse, and at Holmes church, in Northampton. The latter was unique in one respect -- for many years it had only fifteen ladies and not one male member. The men had a perfect Elysium for unregenerate human nature. They had hunting, fishing, oystering, fast horses, public houses and days, and a plenty of that which is said to soothe, and certainly does inebriate. They went to church, talked politics, and supported the Gospel by liberal contributions. But they sadly needed the sermon old Dr. Ross preached in his own church in Huntsville, Ala., to prove that men had souls.

DR. AND MOSES P. HANDY

Rev. Dr. Handy, the prisoner who wrote United States Bonds, giving his experience as a prisoner at Fort Delaware, was then the pastor at Portsmouth. There I met his son, Moses P., who commenced his brilliant journalistic career as a local reporter for the *Dispatch*. Moses was then about

12 years of age, and while very sprightly, his warmest friends could not call him handsome. It may be that the "Gridiron Club," of which he was president, is the result of an evolution from what I knew in college days as the "Ugly Club." The late Dr. Shepperson, also of Hanover, told me he was the standing president of the Ugly Club at Hampden-Sidney [sic] , without opposition. At last, the late Judge F. N. Watkins, of Farmville, announced himself a candidate. The contest was so close that it was decided that each candidate should stick his head through a horse-collar as a frame. "But," said the Doctor, "as soon as I put my head through the collar Frank Nat gave it up."

But, to return. Moses, at that time, as some other preachers' sons I know of, had been destined by his father for the ministry. He wrote a sermon, shown me by his father, and while I cannot remember my own, much less his, I do recall the text, and, I think, the divisions. The text was: "And Job Said," (a) "Who Was Job, Who Said?" (b) "What Did Job Say?" (c) "What Made Job Say What He Said?"

I have crossed the Atlantic four times, but never was sea-sick. Dr. Handy had lived on and near salt-water all his life, and always got sea-sick. I know it is what Sam Jones calls meanness, but I never could help laughing at sea-sickness, especially when a bridal couple, as was the case once, or a brother preacher is the patient. Soon after leaving Old Point I found Dr. Handy stretched out on a lot of whiskey-barrels in the bow, pale as death, but could not help asking him if he was enjoying the fresh air of the salt-breeze or the fumes of the whiskey. He said nothing, but his mute appeals were pathetic.

We went on up to Accomac Courthouse, and one night I spent at "Only Near Onancock", the beautiful home of Governor Wise. Express companies were scarce in those days, and the tenant asked me to carry $200 in gold, as rental to the Governor. I felt like my unknown brother, who borrowed $10 several Saturday nights in succession from one of his deacons, returning it on Monday morning. When asked the meaning of such conduct the poor pastor replied that he never could preach with his pocket-book empty. The deacon took the hint, whether from conscience or a fear of losing his money tradition does not say. But I felt very rich and very much like preaching with all that gold in my pocket.

On my way back to Holmes Church we stopped at an inn, not to get a drink, for I never took a social glass in my life, but to light a cigar. As I looked around the room I was struck with a print hanging on the wall. It looked somewhat like the picture of Lord Byron. It was the Governor, taken when he was a young man and a Whig, and under it was printed that old rallying cry: "The Union of the Whigs, for the sake of the Union." When I handed over the gold to the Governor I felt an almost irresistible impulse

43

to remind him of that picture and that motto. But I remembered that boy at the Rockbridge Baths, and held my peace.

STOLE MY THUNDER

In a sermon at Holmes Church I got off what we college boys used to call "A curl" on the "Old Ship of Zion." At the close of the service a young man borrowed the manuscript, changed the "Old Ship of Zion" to the "Old Ship of State, and made use of it for the Democrats in a pending campaign.

T. W. H.

Article Notes

Henry Clay ran as a Whig for president in 1844 and narrowly lost to James K. Polk, a Democrat.

Henry Alexander Wise of Accomac County served as governor from 1 Jan 1856 to 1 Jan 1860. Wise County is named in his honor as he championed many southwest Virginia causes.

Richmond Dispatch

Richmond, Virginia
Sunday, April 7, 1895

OLD BEULAH CHURCH

LOCATED NEAR COLD HARBOR AND
FOUNDED BY MRS. WOODY

Why and How the Sacred Edifice Came to be Built --
Daily Prayer for a Presbyterian Church Answered

(written for the *Dispatch*)

The whole city of Richmond has recently honored itself by doing honor to Dr. Moses D. Hoge. Together with a great company of younger ministers and other old students of Hampden-Sidney [sic] I love and honor him as Timothy did Paul; and for the same reason. He might say to us, as Paul did to the Corinthians: "For though ye have 10,000 instructors in Christ, yet have ye not many fathers; for in Christ Jesus I have begotten you through the Gospel." Dr. Hoge always reminds me of that stern old Mordecai who sat at the gate of the palace in Shusan, of whom it is written: "But Mordecai bowed not, nor did him reverence." It is not said that Mordecai was a "silver-tongued orator," or any other kind of an orator; but what made him conspicuous was that erect head and unflinching adherence to principle with which he sat erect when the upstart Haman rode by. Dr. Hoge is like "the golden-mouthed Crysostum," as a preacher and if he had the time could write a book that would supersede Dr. Spencer's *Pastor's Sketches*. But, while brotherly and charitable to all, there is a bed-rock of character and moral courage and firmness of theological conviction which has stood the test of fifty years in that one community. Unlike Sidney Smith, who wrote one day that he "did not have energy enough to stick a knife in a dissenter," he has the gentleness of my Uncle Toby, who opened the casement and let out a fly that had been tickling his nose. But the crowds of all denominations who have flocked to his afternoon services know, whether in war or peace, that they will hear a sermon from a southern Presbyterian minister who is never ashamed to say, with Paul, "I am a free-born Roman citizen," whether that meant the Confederate States or the United States, restored by force of arms.

MRS. DAVID WOODY

Not quite a mile from Cold Harbor there lived and died a mother in Israel, who always reminded me of Rispah. Not that she sat on the sackcloth mourning for dead children, but in a very ungodly community she watched her brood of children as they grew up with the keen eye and brave heart of a hen as she eyes the hawk, and the fox, and the mink.

This was Mrs. David Woody [Mary], the founder of Beulah church. She was a sister of the late Dr. John G. Shepperson, and had a great many of the characteristics that made that great and good man so eminent. Soon after the McClellan campaign I published in the *Dispatch* one of her witticisms, whose point by the way, was unfortunately broken off two years later by General Grant. A Yankee major, who had annoyed the family a good deal by insisting on pitching his tent at the door of her chamber, rode up and said; "Ah, Mrs. Woody, we'll have your old rebel capital in a few days; we can see the spires of the churches from our breastworks." "Ah!" said the old lady, with provoking composure, "I read in my Bible that Moses climbed the mountains and saw the Promised Land, but he never got there." On that visit I found the house shot all to pieces, but not a hair of their heads had been touched. I ought to have said she had a husband, but as many of us know, by observation, if not by experience, in this case, at least, the gray mare was so much better than the horse that the home was known as Mrs. Woody's, as though she were a widow. But as I sat and listened to the calm recital of the battle, and asked if they were not alarmed, the old man answered: "Not at all. The same power was taking care of us that always does. A shell struck the chimney and came tumbling down on the fire, but I just got a gourd of water and put out the fuse." Such was the stuff out of which grew that beautiful little church, which became an oasis in the desert.

WHY, AND HOW BUILT

As I have said, my ancestors were Presbyterians from way back, even to the days of Samuel Davies, and were raised near Cold Harbor. So were the Whites and the Watts, and these families seemed to have an elective affinity for each other. Mr. Hugh Watt lived in Hanover, adjoining Powhite, a place which my sister nick-named "Paradise," because Mr. George Watt loved it so well. Mr. George Watt, Sr. lived on Franklin street, near where John Holt Rice preached. These brothers swapped names for their children as they were born; thus George, Jr. was the son of Hugh, and Hugh A. was the son of George.[1] Mrs. Dr. William S. White was a daughter of Mr. George Watt,

1   Hugh and George Watt, sons of Hugh and Margaret Mills Watt, were born in

Sr., and Rev. John Watt was his son. It was Mr. John Watt who caused the Thomasite preacher to jump out of the window of the pulpit and run off by turning his definition of naphesh, the Hebrew word for soul, into ridicule, by quoting in his nasal way, "Why are thou cast down; O, my smelling bottle?" etc.

My father was one of the strongest Presbyterians I ever knew, and when Mr. George Watt was asked how it was that he was a Baptist and my sister a Presbyterian, he immediately gave the solution by saying, "She is Tom Hooper's sister." But, strange to say, I think my father had six sisters, and all of them married Baptists. And, as a general rule, a Baptist who marries

Old Beulah Church. *Pamunkey Woman's Club calendar*, January 1988, by Nan P. Holt. The church was built in 1936.

a Presbyterian sister, as "Club-Ax" Davis, advised, he is like a mud turtle he holds on until it thunders, or until the sister goes down under his native element. At all events, when I was a boy that whole section had drifted off from its old moorings. And when Walnut Grove [Baptist Church] was built, Bethesda was given up to what were then called the Campbellites, or Disciples.

Meantime, more by neglect, perhaps, than bad cultivation on the part of the churches, that section around Cold Harbor became a pandemonium

Glenarm, County Antrim, Ireland. George immigrated to Virginia and Hugh followed sometime afterwards. Both were very successful after their emigration, George as a merchant in Richmond and Hugh as a farmer in Hanover County.

of grog-shops and debauchery. I think the battles around there must have swept these away, for last November, when I went there, after thirty years' absence, I was delighted to find that the desert had been made to blossom as the rose.

THE BUILDER OF BEULAH

For sixteen years, with the persistency and faith of Daniel, and with her windows opened toward Jerusalem, Mrs. Woody and her husband daily prayed for a Presbyterian church. At the end of that time they gave the land for the erection of Beulah, and during my five years of pastoral service there I never missed any member of that family from church at any kind of service.

The late Henry S. Osborn, D. D., was the builder of the first church there, and this was wantonly burned by some of Grant's men in the campaign of 1864 [June 1], as was Pole Green, though the latter was burned in action. He was a bachelor, and had his boarding quarters at the old Washington Henry Academy (established in 1758). Dr. White says this school was started by Samuel Davies, but it must have been before either Washington or Henry became famous, for Mr. Davies left Hanover in 1755 to take the presidency of Nassau Hall College, now Princeton. As intimated before, Mr. Osborn was a universal genius. He drove a curious little top-buggy, with a mare called Dolly, who could make ten miles an hour. Mr. Sidney L. Dunton was principal of the academy, but Mr. Osborn asked my father to let him give me a year's instruction in Latin and Greek before I went to college. I rode a horse named Parson, so called because my father bought him from Rev. Dr. Minnigerode when he moved from the Peninsula to become the beloved rector of St. Paul's. I am glad to say the dear old Doctor was better in his line than the horse was in his, at least as a riding horse. John Stark also rode to school on a small black circus pony who had a trick of lying down in a creek if you let him stop to drink. The negroes said the reason of that was he was born in the month of March. One day Mr. Dunton had a man ploughing near the school-house, and for some cause the horse refused to move. Mr. Dunton and the driver exhausted themselves in useless whippings. Mr. Osborn came out of his study, took in the situation, walked down the path with a small bottle of the spirits of ammonia, and put this to the horse's nose. She turned away at first, but he gave her another whiff, when she walked off as quietly as if she had just been waiting for that spirits of ammonia. He had a way of measuring distances by tying a red rag to the tire of his wheel, and then counting the revolutions of the wheel from place to place and multiplying these by the exact circumference of the wheel.

WAT NOT LONG

Such a restless, energetic pastor was not long in finding out the regions around Cold Harbor and that nest-egg of a Presbyterian church in the Woody family. Time and distance were nothing to him and Dolly, and he would frequently appear at our house for breakfast, and then to use his own expression, "step over" to Richmond, come back by Dr. Gaines's, and hold a prayer-meeting that night at Mrs. Woody's. Dr. Gaines owned a sawmill and readily consented to saw all the timber. Others subscribed so many days of hauling or manual labor, and when the house was well under way Mr. Osborn "stepped over" to Palestine, with Rev. H. Dunning, of Church Hill, and left his old father, Rev. Truman Osborn, to hold the fort while he was gone. The old gentleman was an eccentric genius, and had a way, as some one expressed it, of "slashing around" a text, and he could not bear any interruption. The people were unbroken colts, and had a free and easy way of yawning or shuffling their feet or going in and out at pleasure, which he rebuked. Mrs. Gaines [Jane E. Spindle] asked an old lady once how she liked old Mr. Osborn, and she answered: "Well, tolable; but I'd like him better if he wasn't so rottin tickler."

But the work went on, and by the time I took charge of the church it was one of the most hopeful sections of all that congregation, then extending from the court-house to Cold Harbor. Dr. Gaines's family took special interest, and were always present; he to superintend the Sunday school, the daughters to teach, and Mrs. Gaines to raise the tunes. She did not know one note of music from another. She kept a list of the first lines of familiar hymns on a blank leaf of her hymn-book. I would announce a common metre hymn, and she would run her eyes over her list and say, sometimes in a whisper: "That goes to `Jesus, I Love Thy Charming Name'; or `Am I a Soldier of the Cross,'" and by the time I had finished reading it she would be ready to raise the tune.

FIELD HOSPITAL

In the campaign of 1862 the neat little church was used as a field hospital. The settees had been scattered through the woods by McClellan's forces, the windows were removed, the doors used for amputating tables, and the floor stained with blood. But in a short time we got the house in order, and resumed our services. These continued to the time I left, after Kilpatrick's raid, in [May] 1863. In 1864 it was wantonly burned [by General Philip

49

H. Sheridan and his cavalry on 1 June 1864, the same day that Polegreen Church burned]. Major Robert Stiles and I attended a watermelon feast at Powhite and spoke for the benefit of rebuilding the church. Last November I went there to preach, but the notice had not been given, and the rain continued to fall. But I could not help walking down to the old home of Mrs. Woody, made sacred by a thousand memories. The old man was gone, the old lady was gone, Crissy was gone. Young David, as we called him, now grown as gray as myself, and whom I had ordained an elder, rose with alacrity to greet me, and Mary, bent with rheumatism, turned over in her chair to take my hand. Amid the memories of the blessed dead we knelt together once more in family prayer around that old hearthstone, before which the family sat unmoved and unharmed amid the crash of battle, and from which had gone that spiritual power in other years to build and rebuild Beulah.

THE LAST OF THE QUAKERS

But it is time to close these reminiscences of that goodly land of watermelons and sweet potatoes. Many of the good people there remember the pranks of the quiet boy, who tried experiments on his friends. They all remember how, when 3 years old, he was allowed by his black mammy to go with his older brother and some other boys to see a new straw-cutter in the feed-room of the stable, under the barn. How, with an inquisitive mind, he monkeyed with that machine, and lost the four fingers and end of the thumb of his right hand, leaving him an Ehud, for the rest of his days. They remember how, as a young pastor, he thought he knew it all, and amid their kindly forbearance and sympathy, soon found out that he was a very small specimen of Sir Isaac Newton, who had gathered a few pebbles on the beach, while the great ocean of truth lay before him. To each of these I send greeting, these words written to the last of the Quakers. Along with these old friends of boyhood, the snows of intervening winters have frosted my hair, but I trust they can say with me, "Goodness and mercy have followed me all the days of my life," and may each of us be able, through the same grace, to say, "And I will dwell in the house of the Lord forever."

To understand the allusion in the following letter, copied by my request from the printed slip pasted in "Aunt Lou's Bible," I must explain. I always loved the Quakers, the Crenshaws, Clarks, etc., of Hanover, and the Pleasants, Whitlocks, and Bates of Richmond. One of the few small vices of my dear old mother was a fondness for "Maccaboy snuff." Her snuff-box was always in her work-basket, and I was fond of taking a pinch, which always gave me away by making me sneeze, which she never did. This I turned to good account, and the "token" alluded to in the letter was a small silver-plated snuff-box, with the name and date engraved on the lid.

When I moved to Lynchburg I found a widowed member of my church and her widowed sister living with their Aunt Lou, an aged and very timid, and shrinking Quakeress. On several visits she quietly declined to receive men into her chamber. But, at last assured that I was one of those free and easy kind of preachers who did not put on uppish airs, she consented. I found her sitting in the corner of the fireplace, knitting, as my mother used to do. As the other ladies and I carried on a sprightly conversation, I caught the old lady slipping her snuff-box out of her basket to take a pinch. I arose and took one with her, and thus sealed the warmest friendship, which lasted as long as she lived. The following clipping from the *Lynchburg News* will explain the rest and close these reminiscences, at least for the present, amid which I have been living for many weeks:

CONGRATULATIONS FROM
REV. T. W. HOOPER, D. D.

Last Sunday's issue of the News contained a paragraph under the caption, "Interesting Reminiscences," referring in brief to several aged and prominent residents of Lynchburg, among them Miss Louisa Davis, who had celebrated her 93rd birthday. The article in the News was read by our former esteemed townsman, Rev. T. W. Hooper, D. D., who for several years was the beloved pastor of the Second Presbyterian church in this city, and the following interesting letter suggested by its perusal was received a few days ago:

Selma, Ala., March 6, 1888

Miss Louisa Davis:

My Beloved Friend, -- The News, which came this morning, told me that on last Lords-day thou didst see the 93rd anniversary of thy birth. The mere mention of thy name brought back some of the sweetest memories of other days. I was sitting by thee in the old chamber, watching thy sweet face, smelling the aroma of thy snuff-box, and listening to thy gentle voice, telling me of the good old days at the Quaker meeting-house. The memory was so sweet, and the fact that our common Friend has been so kind and loving to thee and thine so long, I could not restrain the impulse of my loving heart. So I will send thee a small token by mail, that may call to mind one who hath often thought of thee amid the silence of many years. Thy pilgrimage hath been long and varied, but softly the dew of God's grace hath fallen on thy heart, and gladsome hath been the sunshine that hath made the dewdrops sparkle along thy pathway.

Now thou art old and feeble, the same arm that hath sustained thee so long is as strong and unwearied as ever, and the rest that remaineth to an aged saint must seem very sweet to thee, when the grapes of Eschol are ripe and luscious to the taste even here.

The Lord bless thee, and keep thee; the Lord make His face shine upon thee, and be gracious unto thee; the Lord lift up His countenance upon thee, and give thee peace."

Thy old friend,
T. W. Hooper

MORE GLEANINGS

THE TWO HOUSES
A CONTRAST – ECCLESIASTES 7:2

By Rev. T. W. Hooper, D.D.

My short visit to the Belfast Council was buried by the approaching marriage of a sister. Meeting me in New York, the wife of twenty-five years, renewed our youth, with what we are pleased to call our "bridal trip." With an elder in the city and a deacon, whose summer house is at Sea Bright, to show us all kindly attention, never, perhaps, were a pastor and bride so delightfully entertained. Leaving there after a few days of unalloyed happiness, we came on by way of Baltimore, Norfolk and Lynchburg, to the beautiful home of my brother [William Davis Hooper], which is called "Fancy Farm," and lies at the very base of the Peaks of Otter.

Here we were greeted by every member that survives of my father's large family, with the addition of nearly a dozen nephews and nieces. For several days we enjoyed all that such a reunion could contribute to a family, separated by years and with an ocean intervening. On Tuesday, the groom, escorted by his old professor colleague at Emory and Henry College, came in; and while the ladies were busy in the house, we gentlemen sat out under the shade of the grand old oaks, while children of all ages romped from house to yard, keenly alive to the novel sensations of a marriage in the country. Among these children were little Willie, the son of Manfred and Bettie Call, of Richmond, Va. He was a beautiful child, of that singular angelic beauty which artist love to look upon as models of the ideals that float in poetic fancies. With clusters of golden curls, eyes as blue as the sky of Italy, cheeks as rosy as the bloom of a ripe peach, lips red and parted always with a baby smile, he was indeed, the prettiest child I ever saw; in nature, or on canvas.

The morning glided away, and after the marriage and the sumptuous dinner, we parted; and "the House of Feasting" sank back to its rural quiet and beauty.

A few weeks had scattered us to all quarters of the compass, leaving the sweetest memories of our late reunion. But what a change has come over the happy summer home? Little Willie is gone to a home that is ten thousand times fairer than that. Allowed to play with some shattered wheat, he swallowed some grains, and without knowing the cause, all that medical skill and sleepless attention could do was done to relieve him. The inflammation was relieved, but some of the chaff had lodged in the wind-pipe and lungs; and at last, while sleeping in the arms of the young mother, he breathed out his young life so quietly, that they thought he was still asleep.

And now, in Hollywood, the marble casket that rivaled all the genius of Raphael or Michelangelo, sleeps beneath the sod, while the more beautiful soul, a ransomed spirit, is at rest.

At such a time and now while the mother, in tearless, sleepless, speechless grief, is hanging in suspense between a life which looks so blank and a death which would reunite, it may seem like a hollow mockery to hear these words: "It is better to go to the house of mourning than to go to the house of feasting; for that is the end of all men; and the living will lay it to his heart."

But these words are what God himself has written, and the time will come when, through grace, they will all see and feel that they are true. Death is not the greatest mystery that confronts us in "the ways of God," for sometimes there is such a thing as "a living death," even with a child. The death of a child is a dagger driven through the heart and leaves a scar, which never vanishes. But the death of a child opens the door of heaven, and makes the songs of angels, and is as wonderful, and in some respects, is a more wonderful display of God's redeeming and converting grace, than the conversion of Saul or the death of Stephen.

And merry and bright and happy as was that summer home on that cloudless summer day when the marriage bells were ringing; it was brighter still when the angels came at sunrise, and took little Willie from his mother's arms and put him "safe in the arms of Jesus," while all the bells of heaven rang out the welcome to another ransomed soul.

[William Hooper (Willie) Call b. 4 Feb 1882, Richmond, VA – d. 7 Sep 1884, Bedford Co., VA - Fancy Farm, buried Hollywood Cemetery, son of Manfred and Sarah Elizabeth Watt Call.

On the next page is the obituary of Mrs. Elizabeth Carleton (Haw) Hooper who died in Richmond, Va. Her residence in 1879 was 103 N. 3rd Street. She was buried at Beaver Dam Farm in Hanover County, Va. The Hooper family was disinterred and reinterred in the George Watt family plot in Hollywood Cemetery, Richmond, Va.]

Obituary
In Memoriam

HOOPER – December 24, 1879, Mrs. Elizabeth Carleton [Haw] Hooper, widow of Mr. Joseph Hooper, an honored elder of the Presbyterian church in Hanover county, Va., and the mother of Rev. T. W. Hooper, D.D., of Selma, Ala.

Rarely have severer trials than here, fallen to the lot of one of God's people; and still more rarely have such trials been so patiently borne. At one time bereaved within a few months of three lovely and promising children, one of them just verging upon manhood; at another deprived by one stroke of a beloved and devoted husband and a comfortable and cherished home; and later in life called upon to mourn the loss of a most affectionate and tenderly loved daughter, whose rare loveliness of character and manners won all hearts. Mrs. Hooper was never known to murmur or repine. Though weeping quietly, silently for her husband and children through all the long years, which followed their loss, she wept not as one without hope, but ever looked trustingly, cheerfully forward to meeting them again in a higher and better world.

Nor were her trials without alleviation. To her were granted in large measure the consolation of the Holy Spirit, and the loving sympathy of Christian friends. The respectful and affectionate deportment and the thoughtful attentions of devoted children, soothed and cheered her declining years. And to her was granted the greatest blessing a Christian mother can know – that of seeing all her children within the fold of the Church – one of them in the ministry, and all of them filling their places well in the Church and in the world.

Thus sustained and comforted, she lived out serenely, even cheerfully, her allotted three-score years and ten; and on Christmas Eve, when all Christendom was preparing to celebrate with rejoicing the coming of the Saviour, she went to meet him in the New Jerusalem, and tossing her songs of joy and praise among the angels of God.

Never was any death-bed more completely robbed of terrors. Through a living faith in her Redeemer, she met death not only serenely, but joyously, "I would not live longer; I esteem it a privilege to die," were among her last words. "Blessed are the dead who die in the Lord."

"Thanks be to God who giveth us the victory through our Lord Jesus Christ."

Note: The previous Tom Hooper articles have provided good insight into the life and times of the eastern part of Hanover County. The following articles by Mr. Joseph R. Haw, Hampton and his sister, Miss Mary Jane Haw, expand upon Rev. Hooper's during the same period.

Mr. Haw's articles have been copied from *The Confederate Veteran Magazine*, 1925, Volume XXXIII, pages 256-258, 340-341 and 373-376 and Miss Haw's from the *Christian Observer*, May 18, 1910, Volume 9, Number 20, pages 22-23.

HAW'S SHOP COMMUNITY OF VIRGINIA

By Joseph R. Haw, Hampton, VA

Early in the nineteenth century, John Haw, III, began the manufacture of farming and milling machinery at the east end of his farm, where the road to Hanover Courthouse crosses the Richmond Road The water power at the mill, which was only a mile from the shop, was used to drive the saw mill, foundry, and the machine shop until, a fire having destroyed the mill, steam power was substituted for water power and the machinery moved up to the crossroads. Not being daunted by adversity, John Haw pushed his work ahead, adding to his plant equipment and skilled labor as business increased until, between 1850-60, he was fully prepared to compete with any similar plant in the State.

At this time Tidewater Virginia was at high-water mark of financial and social prosperity. Mr. Edmund Ruffin, one of the best theoretical and practical farmers in the whole South, had introduced improved methods of farming, and the abundance of green sand, marl, and oyster shell lime freely applied to the river lands had so increased their fertility that, to quote Mr. Ruffin, "seventeen million dollars were added to the assessed value of the land in this section between the years 1830-50." Wheat, the principal money crop, found a ready market at Richmond Flouring Mills, at that time probably the equal of any in the world. The flour made by them of this wheat was preferred above all others by South America and Australia, as it stood the long sea voyage better than any other flour made in America. The farms were very large, and each farmer endeavored to have his farm fully equipped with all the machinery necessary to build and keep up repairs and prepare all of his crops for market, such as sawmills, grist mills, threshers, etc. John Haw had won the confidence of the Tidewater farmers and other districts, and prospects were very bright in 1860-61 for the shop. Orders were booked to keep it running at full capacity for the 1861 season, and peace and prosperity reigned. Three sons of John Haw and one of his nephews were employed in this plant. His skilled workmen and apprentices were from highly respectable families, mostly well-to-do farmers of strict integrity, who, after giving their sons the benefit of such private schools as were available, preferred to give them a trade rather than a profession of doubtful utility.

The Haw's Shop Community was exceptionally temperate, law abiding, and patriotic. There was a Presbyterian Church, Salem, and a schoolhouse at the Shop; and, one mile farther on the Richmond Road, Enon Methodist Church.

The schoolhouse had been built for a Temperance Hall in the time of the noted John B. Gough, temperance lecturer. Salem Church membership had been moved up from Hanovertown, a colonial port for shipping tobacco, and no doubt its members had in early days listened to the stirring eloquence of Samuel Davies, the pioneer dissenter, whose eloquence and fervent patriotism so inspired Patrick Henry. The pastors of the Church were men of refinement and education. One of them, Henry Osborn, becoming a college professor and writer of note on scientific subjects.

Several years before the War between the States, the Rev. Tom Hooper, a nephew of John Haw, a brilliant young preacher, became pastor of this Church, and his earnest manner, fine address, and excellent delivery drew many to hear him, among them some of the elite of the land. On the Sabbath day the church and churchyard would present an interesting picture when the fine, silver-mounted coaches, drawn by slick, highly bred horses, shining in silver-mounted harness, drove up near the door to deliver their precious load of feminine beauty. There was the Courthouse contingent from the Courtland Estate, William O. Winston, his wife and two handsome daughters, Miss Betty, soon to become the bride of the handsome, gallant, dashing cavalry officer, Gen. Thomas L. Rosser; and Miss Sally, equally as pretty and attractive. The Signal Hill family of Bickerton Winston, his wife (who was Miss [Elizabeth Minor] Bankhead) and daughters, Misses Margaret and Janey, the latter to become the wife of Major Waldow, of Savannah, Ga., a gallant cavalry officer; and the Dundee cavalcade led by the head of the house, Dr. Lucian Price, mounted on his well-groomed, spirited black steed, followed by the family coach containing Mrs. [Ellen M.] Price, the English governess, and daughters, Misses Lizzie and Nannie, the former soon to become the wife of Dr. Johnny Fontaine, Jeb Stuart's medical director, who, after a short, brilliant career, lost his life while ministering to the mortally wounded General Donavant [Dunovant] on the field of battle. Following the carriage came the large bus drawn by a team of four, bearing the select boarders of the Dundee Private School, a bevy of handsome girls. Nearer the church may be mentioned the [George W.] Pollards, of Williamsville, the Doctor and his accomplished wife [Mary P. Todd] and daughter, Miss Ellen, afterwards Mrs. Converse, of Louisville, Ky.; and the widow [Mrs. William T. H., Susan C.] Pollard, from Buckeye, with her charming, curly-headed girls; not to mention many others and the cavalcade of gallant young men, who rode after the carriages on horseback.

After John Brown's invasion of Virginia in October, 1859, this abortive forerunner of what the people of the South were to expect from the Grand Old Party acted as a bugle call to arms, and in every community volunteer companies were formed. Among them the Hanover Grays [Company I, 15th Virginia Infantry], made up of the men of the lower of Hanover County, including the Haw's Shop Community.

In the exciting presidential election campaign of 1860, the schoolhouse was used as a "Bell and Everett Clubhouse," and a flag bearing their names was unfurled to the breeze. Weekly meetings were held and there were warm debates between Democrats of the Calhoun and Yancey following, who championed the Breckinridge and Lane ticket and secession, and the Bell and Everett followers, who stood for the Union and the Constitution. On one occasion a Bell and Everett speaker asked his opponent if the South seceded what would they do for arms of defense, as the South had no supply. His opponent answered promptly with great vehemence; "We will fight them with flintlock muskets and double-barrelled shotguns, and, if these give out, we will fight them with these things that God Almighty gave us (shaking both fists in a most belligerent manner), until we wear them off up to the elbows." He never fired a gun nor volunteered.

At the election, John Haw, an Old Line Whig, his twin sons, and his nephew, R. W. Haw, voted the Bell and Everett ticket, the three last casting their first vote. Most of the shop employees eligible voted the same ticket, thus entering their protest against the rash act of secession and helping to carry the State for this conservative ticket. The next six months were filled with anxiety and suspense. The Southern States having seceded, Lincoln called for 75,000 troops to coerce the South, and Virginia cast her lot with the Confederacy.

When the Hanover Grays reached the Peninsula [May, 1861] and went into camp, news was received that they were without tents or shelter of any kind. The schoolhouse and churchyard became a scene of activity. A meeting was held, and a committee of one appointed to go to Richmond to buy tent cloth, take the measure of the proper sized tents, and report. The cloth having arrived, the busy hands of the ladies of the community soon had very good wall tents made, which added much to the comfort of the boys.

In the meantime, the first battle of the war had been fought on the Peninsula at Big Bethel [June 10, 1861], but no particulars as to the casualties could be had, so with much anxiety and tears the tent making went on to completion. Scarcely were the tents shipped when an earnest call came from the Richmond hospitals asking to be relieved of their convalescent patients. The community rallied at once to meet their very urgent demand.

The schoolhouse was converted into a very comfortable hospital ward, and another building near into a dining room and kitchen.

Farmers supplied abundant provisions, such as fresh lamb, mutton, chickens, hams, eggs, vegetables, fruits, and milk. Competent negro cooks prepared the food, supervised by matchless Virginia housewives of the community. Young ladies brought flowers to adorn the wards and sang the popular songs of the day to cheer the homesick lads. The memory of those pleasant days of convalescence clung to some of the lads through all the strenuous days of the war, and from their far Southern homes they recalled the scenes and heard again the songs sung by the maidens of this community.

John Haw and his wife [Mary Austin Watt], a Christian woman of remarkable executive ability, not only contributed liberally to the community hospital both time and material, but cared for convalescents all through the summer and fall at Oak Grove their hospitable home, bringing them out from the St. Charles Hotel Hospital in Richmond and returning them when they had recuperated.

In the spring [May] of 1862, McClellan landed his great army at Fortress Monroe, marched up the Peninsula, and besieged Richmond. His cavalry established a picket post at Haw's Shop to protect the right flank of his army. In June, Jeb Stuart surprised his picket post by capturing the vidette near Oak Grove, chased the company back on the regiment, routed it, and rode around McClellan's army. On the 27th of the same month, the battle of Cold Harbor, sometimes called Gaines' Mill fought mainly on Springfield, the Watt Farm. Mrs. Sarah Bohanan [Bohannon] Kidd Watt, a widow over seventy-five years old and sick in bed, was carried to a place of safety, the house taken for a Yankee hospital and filled with wounded. Mrs. Watt never returned to her home. She died in a few months at Oak Grove, the home of her daughter, Mrs. John Haw.

When the Haw boys volunteered and entered the Southern army, Haw's Shop was closed down, as nearly all of the white employees entered the service. It was suggested that the machinery be moved to Richmond and that John Haw have the men detailed and manufacture ammunition for the government. To this his sons would not agree, as it was thought by the men at the front to be cowardly to serve in what were called "bombproof" positions. Realizing that this valuable property would be destroyed by the enemy, John Haw, after McClellan had retired, sold it to the Tredegar Works of Richmond. Failing to invest the money in valuable real estate or other sound property, it was a total loss. Repeated raids by Stoneman, Spiers, Kilpatrick, Sheridan, the cavalry battle of Haw's Shop, and Grant's army swept the farm of everything worth taking -- fences, crops, horses, mules, cows, hogs, chickens, turkeys, and vehicles -- nothing was lacking to make the farm a barren desert but the sowing of salt on the land. The Tidewater District, once so prosperous, was now prostrate in poverty.

How John Haw and his boys and former employees returned to their homes, devoted themselves to the task of redeeming the land, helping to rout the scalawags and carpetbaggers and bring the land back to its fertility and productiveness is but the story of the whole section. The task was hard and strenuous. Many fell by the way, not equal to the strain; but Tidewater Virginia is again prosperous and her present generation true to the faith of the fathers.

THE HAW BOYS IN THE WAR BETWEEN THE STATES

attributed to
Joseph Richardson Haw

Tradition says John Haw, the immigrant, ran away from his home in England and came to America because his parents wished him to become a preacher. He landed in Eastern Virginia and, after varied experiences, married a Miss [Elizabeth] Carleton and settled on Oak Grove Farm, in Hanover County, adjoining Studley, the birthplace of Patrick Henry. He died about the beginning of the Revolutionary War, leaving as heir one son, John Haw II, who, dying early in the nineteenth century, left two sons, minors, John Haw III, and Richardson Tyre [Tyree] Haw, also a daughter. John Haw III fell heir to Oak Grove Farm and a water mill for grinding corn, and Richardson T. Haw to a farm [Locust Hill] one mile from Oak Grove.

Late in the eighteenth century there arrived in Richmond, Va., four members of the Watt family from the North of Ireland. The two brothers, George and Hugh, remained in Richmond as merchants, while the two sisters settled in Pennsylvania, where Pittsburgh now stands. Hugh Watt married Sarah Bohanan Kidd and moved to her farm, Springfield, on the Chickahominy River, in Hanover County, eight miles from Richmond. The hardest part of the first battle of Cold Harbor, 1862, was fought on this farm. John Haw III married Mary Austin Watt, daughter of Hugh Watt, and Richardson Haw married Margaret Mills Watt, her sister. As a result of these marriages, there were children of John and Mary A. Haw, two daughters and five sons; of Richardson and Margaret Haw, seven daughters and two sons. When the presidential election of 1860 occurred, Richardson Haw having died, there remained only eight male representatives of the Haw family in America. When the War Between the States ended, six of these had served in the Confederate army; one, John Haw, being too old, and one, John Osborn Haw, too young. In the group picture are the four brothers, sons of John and Mary Austin Watt Haw; in the lower row are John Hugh and George Pitman Haw, twins, born July, 1838, and still living in their eighty-seventh year. In the upper row are Joseph R. Haw, born December,1845, now in his eightieth year, and William Haw, born September, 1840, who died at Ashland, Va., in August, 1911. The single picture is of Edwin Haw, born December, 1843; died March, 1874. The one in uniform is Richardson Wallace Haw, son of Richardson and Margaret Haw, born May, 1838, and died in Chesterfield County, November, 1901. John H. and George P. Haw, twins, William, their brother, and Richardson Haw, their double first cousin, were members of the Hanover Grays.

Four Haw Brothers Front row, L-R: John Hugh, George Pittman, Back row, L-R: Joseph R., William, Source: *15th VA Infantry* by Louis H. Manarin.

William Haw   Edwin Haw   Richardson Haw

When Virginia seceded, the Hanover Grays entered the service of the State on the 23rd of April, 1861, and later became Company I of the 15th Virginia Infantry, serving under Gen. Bankhead Magruder on the Virginia Peninsula. With not more than 11,500 men General Magruder defeated General Butler at Big Bethel, then fortified and held a defensive line of fourteen miles against McClellan with the Grand Army of the Potomac, 118,000 strong, until Gen. Joseph E. Johnston arrived. The regiment fought at Dam No. 1, Williamsburg, and Barramsville. In the seven days fighting in 1862, Magruder held the thin line around Richmond while General Lee, with Hill, Longstreet, Jackson, and others, executed the flank movement which relieved Richmond and defeated McClellan, the regiment fighting at Malvern Hill and at Sharpsburg.

In the retreat from the Peninsula to Richmond, John H. Haw was taken with a severe case of typhoid fever and was unfit for duty for a year. George P. Haw was elected first lieutenant in 1862 and commanded the company at Sharpsburg, it being then in Semmes's Brigade, McLaw's Division. Worn down by long marches, the company was reduced to sixteen men, and Lieutenant Haw was its only officer present. Three were killed and eleven wounded, Lieut. George P. Haw losing his left arm.

After the Battle of Fredericksburg, December, 1862, the regiment was put in Corse's Brigade, Pickett's Division, and went with Longstreet on the Suffolk expedition in the winter of 1862-63, gathering supplies for the army. The men suffered a great deal from exposure, being poorly supplied with shoes and clothing, many being barefooted. In 1863 the brigade defended General Lee's communications in Virginia until after the Battle of Gettysburg. It captured and held Manassas and Chester Gap, securing a safe retreat for General Lee's army.

The winter of 1863-64 the brigade spent in an active campaign in Southwest Virginia and Tennessee, protecting Longstreet's communications, marching through sleet and snow, wading frozen rivers, many of them barefooted, the frozen roads cutting the blood from their feet, and camping with no shelter save the canopy of heaven.

In 1864 the brigade fought at New Bern, N. C., and, on May 16, at Drewry's Bluff where Ben Butler was whipped; then with Lee at Hanover Junction, Cold Harbor, and the capture of the Howlett House Line; in 1865 it fought Sheridan at Ashland, Dinwiddie Courthouse, Five Forks, and Sailor's Creek. After the loss of his arm, Lieut. George P. Haw was assigned to light duty as conscript officer in his native county of Hanover, Va.

John H. Haw returned to his company early in 1864, and, as first sergeant, was with his command in the Tennessee and North Carolina campaigns, and fought at Drewry's Bluff, Hanover Junction, Cold Harbor, and the Howlett House; was then transferred to the ordnance department at Selma, Ala Navy Yard, where large siege guns were made of the fine Alabama iron for the navy and coast defense.

Sergt. William Haw was wounded at Drewry's Bluff, and at Five Forks was shot through both arms and his body just below the heart, captured, and remained in a Yankee prison hospital at Newport News until August, 1865. He was a splendid soldier and never absent from his command except on account of sickness or wounds.

Edwin Haw joined the regiment in the fall of 1864, took part in the fighting at Ashland, Va., Five Forks, and Sailor's Creek; was wounded at Five Forks, and paroled at Lynchburg, April 13, 1865.

Richardson W. Haw served through the whole war in the regiment and surrendered at Appomattox; was wounded at Drewry's Bluff. When the war ended, he was brevet lieutenant in charge of the ambulance corps of his regiment.

Joseph R. Haw, the youngest of the five sons, entered the service September, 1863; was assigned to the ordnance department and employed in the C.S.A. Armory at Richmond, where the Harper's Ferry machinery had been installed for making rifles. All civilian employees of the government were put on a military footing and into battalions and a brigade under Gen. G.W.C. Lee for the protection of Richmond. The brigade was ordered out on many occasions to meet raids, and, in September, 1864, manned the works in front of Fort Harrison, which had been captured by the Yankees and held by them. On the 1st of March, 1864, the brigade met and defeated a detachment of Kilpatrick's command under Dahlgren, inside the outer works near West Hampton. Only three battalions came up in time to take part in the fighting, the first, or Armory Battalion, Scrugg's Battalion, and Henley's Battalion. The first battalion was more than a mile in advance of the brigade and met the enemy, double their number, and checked them, giving time for the next two battalions to form a safe line of battle. Joseph R. Haw, a member of Company A, 1st Battalion, was with his command in this fight and did his part faithfully also in the lines in front of Fort Harrison, where the constant picket duty in a flooded swamp for four months was very trying. On the evacuation of Richmond, Sunday, April 2, 1865, the employees of the ordnance department were ordered to take the train for Danville, Va. A small number assembled at the depot, Joseph R. Haw among them, and took a freight train loaded with ordnance supplies (bullet molds, lead, etc.), past midnight, arriving at Danville on the 3rd after dark. J. R. Haw remained in Danville until General Lee surrendered; then, with a comrade, Albert Cuthbert, of Georgia, a member of the Jeff Davis Legion, walked to Bush Hill, near High Point, N. C., sixty-five miles, where he met with and joined Company A, 4th Tennessee (Shaw's)Battalion, Dibrell's Brigade, Dibrell's Division escort to President Davis; marched with them to Washington, Ga., where he was paid off in silver and gold and paroled May 10, 1865. He received $25.75.

Three of Richardson Tyre [Tyree] Haw's daughters -- Sally Kidd, Cornelia, and Helen Marr -- were matrons in Camp Winder Hospital, and six of them married men in the Confederate service.

At the close of the war George P. Haw entered the law class at Washington College, now Washington and Lee University, and graduated in 1867. His diploma, signed by Gen. R. E. Lee, President is one of his most cherished possessions. He was Commonwealth Attorney for Hanover County for more than thirty years, retiring from a lucrative practice a few years ago. Now in his eighty-seventh year, he resides with a devoted daughter at Dundee, still attending and working in the Samuel Davies Group of Presbyterian Churches, of which he has been an active ruling elder for more than sixty years. Enjoying the society of his children and grandchildren, looking back without regret on a well-spent life full of earnest work and accomplishments, with the love and esteem of neighbors and friends.

John H. and William Haw, assisted by their father, leased the site of Putney Mills on the Pamunkey River (Sheridan having burned the mill), rebuilt the mill and a machine shop, and carried on this work for some years, rebuilding burned mills and contracting. They then dissolved partnership. John H. Haw purchased the Old Piping Tree Farm and Ferry on the Pamunkey River and became a farmer. Quoting from a Richmond paper: "He has eschewed both politics and matrimony, but he is a mighty fox hunter, having more than a State-wide reputation, and the hounds raised at his kennels stand ace high in sporting circles. Until a few years ago he used to give house parties for his young relatives and their friends, invitations to which were highly valued." He is still active in his eighty-seventh year.

Joseph R. Haw, entered the Virginia Agricultural and Mechanical College, now the Virginia Polytechnic Institute, in 1874, and graduated in 1876 in the full course of agriculture and mechanics; then spent one year as postgraduate and instructor. He was employed as foreman and superintendent in machine shops and as civil engineer on railroad construction until 1896, when he entered the Quartermaster Department, U. S. A., at Fort Monroe, Va., as engineer in classified service; was retired under the Civil Service in 1922; was married in 1891 to Miss Mamie Cumming, and has one son, Maj. Joseph C. Haw, West Point Military Academy, Class 1915, Coast Artillery Corp. U. S. A. He now resides in Hampton, Va., and is quite active for seventy-nine years.

THE BATTLE OF HAW'S SHOP, VA.

By Joseph R. Haw , Hampton, Va..

Was the battle of Haw's Shop the hardest cavalry fight of the war in Virginia?

The cavalry with Grant's army, April, 1864, commanded by Gen. Philip H. Sheridan, consisted of three divisions -- [Alfred T. A.] Torbert's, D. M. Grey's, and [James H.] Wilson's -- thirty-two regiments of 12,424 men, not including 1,812 cavalry attached to the Ninth Corps, nor horse artillery acting with the corps. They were equipped with sabers, revolvers, and breech-loading repeating carbines. On Sheridan's first raid [Beaver Dam Depot, 9 May 1864], in the spring of 1864, his column was thirteen miles long. Grant's plan of campaign from the Rapidan to Appomattox was a continual movement from his right flank to his left. Sheridan, with this heavy force of cavalry, moved ahead, securing new positions for the infantry. He was always met by the Confederate cavalry, under General Stuart, and, after his death, under Hampton and Fitz Lee, when very heavy fighting was done by the cavalry, which was almost constantly engaged until the end of the campaign at Appomattox.

When Grant, after fighting the battles of the Wilderness and Spotsylvania, moved down to the head of the waters of the Pamunkey River, on the North Anna River [Battle of North Anna, May 23-26, 1864], he found General Lee in a fine position, too formidable to assault. He therefore moved down the north coast side of the Pamunkey River, with Sheridan in advance, about fifteen miles or more, to Hanovertown Ferry.

On the 27th of May, Sheridan crossed the Pamunkey and drove in a Maryland regiment under Gen. Bradley T. Johnson, had a sharp fight with Gordon's Brigade of North Carolina Cavalry, and marched up the Richmond Road four miles to Haw's Shop and Farm about sixteen miles from Richmond, and posted a strong picket at Enon Church, one mile past the shop.

The Richmond and Hanovertown Road is crossed at Haw's Shop by a county road leading from Hanover Courthouse, following the general direction of the river to lower ferries, New Castle and the White House, and to Cold Harbor. Besides the steam grist mill and sawmill, foundry and machine shop, known as Haw's Shop, there was the Salem Presbyterian Church, a schoolhouse, and several residences, while Oak Grove, the Haw residence, was half a mile farther on the road, half way between the shop and Enon Church, the farm fronting the Richmond Road a mile. On the morning of the 28th of May, General Hampton, with Fitz Lee's Division, his

69

own division, and General Butler's Brigade of South Carolina Cavalry, moved on the Richmond Road to Enon Church and attacked the Yankees.

The men dismounted and formed a line of battle across the road at right angles, protecting themselves as best they could behind the trees and any other available objects at hand. The position was a very strong one for the Confederates. There were two creeks running into the Pamunkey River, about four miles apart where they entered the river, Crump's Creek north of Hanovertown Ferry and the Totopotomoy south of it. The Richmond Road at Enon Church runs on a divide between two small streams. On the Confederate left, the southern branch of Crump's Creek ran nearly parallel to the road, turning to the left where there had

Salem Church, *Pamunkey Woman's Club Calendar*, January 1986, by Janet Ogden Thompson.

been a mill pond. Its banks were covered with timber and underbrush, and the site of the mill pond was a flooded marsh almost impassable. On their right a north branch of the Totopotomoy ran parallel to the road and then bore to the right and entered Haw's Mill Pond. Stream and pond were flanked by timber and underbrush. Gen. W. H. F. Lee, with his division, or a part of it, held the Confederate left northeast side the southern branch, separated by the stream from Hampton and Lee. The entire battle raged between these streams. The Confederates had the advantage of the forest almost the entire length of the battle line, while the Yankees had forest on the right of the road, but field and small scrub pines on the left. The length between streams was hardly a mile.

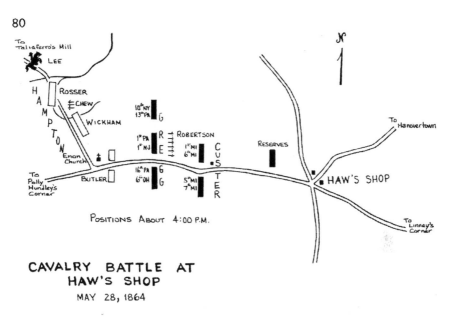

CAVALRY BATTLE AT HAW'S SHOP
MAY 28, 1864

Military Operations in Hanover County, Virginia: 1861-1865, by John M. Gabbert, p. 80.

General [Williams C.] Wickham's brigade of Virginia troops, after fighting for some time, was relieved by [Matthew C.] Butler's South Carolinians. The Virginians, though veteran troops, suffered a good deal in killed and wounded. Butler's brigade, consisting of the 4th, 5th, and 6th South Carolina Cavalry, had just arrived from South Carolina and were unaccustomed to severe fighting at close range and had not learned to protect themselves. On reaching the battle field, they went in with a yell, thus revealing their presence to the enemy. They were armed with the English Enfield Rifle, muzzle loaders, which required much more exposure of the body in leading than the breech-loading carbines. Sergt. Robert Hudgins, of Wickham's Brigade, who is still living, says he never saw so many men wounded in the arm in his experience during the war as in this fight. General [J.E.B.] Stuart, in a dispatch to Richmond, just previous to this, said of the Yankee cavalry: "They are armed with breech-loading repeating carbines, and fight much better than their infantry." From official records we find that the Second Division, commanded by Brig. Gen. McGregg, of two brigades, and Custer's Michigan Brigade, did the fighting on this part of the line. [Wesley] Merritt's Brigade, of the First Division, was on the Yankee right, as was also [Thomas C.] Devin's Brigade. Sheridan

71

claims he fought the whole Confederate Cavalry Corps and drove them from their breastworks. He says: "This was a hard-contested engagement, with heavy loss for the number of troops engaged on both sides. These Carolinians fought very gallantly in this their first fight, judging from the dead, wounded, and captured. The most determined efforts were made on both sides and neither would give way until late in the afternoon, when Custer's Brigade, of four regiments, dismounted and charged, driving the enemy out of his works."

Custer says his regiment gave ground several times under cross fire from the Confederates, and that the havoc was particularly great in Butler's Brigade of South Carolina Cavalry; that his own loss was greater than in any other engagement of the campaign. His personal aide had the end of his thumb shot off and a dangerous wound in his thigh, and his horse shot under him, and another member of his staff had his horse killed. He also says the 5th Michigan Regiment was armed with the Spencer seven-shooting breech-loading rifles, and he thinks them the best rifle in the army for cavalry.

Gen. Henry E. Davis, commanding the First Brigade, Second Division, U.S.A., said: "Very severe engagement, lasting seven hours." John W. Keester, commanding the 1st New Jersey Cavalry: "The enemy directed his fire to this part of the line, and the severest cavalry fight of the war waged for two hours in my front. The enemy were South Carolinians, armed with Enfield rifles, and were very formidable." Col. Russell A. Alger, who commanded the 5th Michigan Regiment, reports that his regiment fought hand to hand, in small pines to the left of the road. He also makes the following statement: "I regret to report that John A. Huff, Company E, the man mentioned who wounded Gen. J.E.B. Stuart at Yellow Tavern, on the 11th of May, 1864, has recently died of wounds received at Haw's Shop, May 28. He had belonged to Berdon's Sharpshooters two years and won the prize as best shot in the regiment. He was forty-eight years of age and lived at Armada, Mich." Colonel Alger was Secretary of War under McKinley. In his *Regimental Losses of the Civil War, 1861-1865*, Fox gives as the greatest losses in killed and wounded at Haw's Shop more than a third of the 5th Michigan and one-fourth killed and wounded of the 6th Michigan.

In the August [*Confederate*] *Veteran* of 1916 there is a very interesting sketch of the life of Captain Pinckney, in which the author says of the 4th South Carolina Regiment: "They arrived at Richmond May 24, 1864, and in the engagement at Haw's Shop, May 28, where so many Charlestonians, especially members of the Light Dragoons, gave up their lives for their country, Captain Pinckney was cut off from his command and taken prisoner. Although he was reported as killed, he was able to get through the lines a message to his family, which was forwarded by Capt. Rawlins Lownds of Hampton's staff. Of the Charleston Dragoons, it was said that out of thirty-six at Haw's Shop they had nine killed and eleven wounded; at Cold Harbor, half of those in action; and at Trevillians, again half. That at the close of the war the company had not more than ten men. I have been unable to find Wade Hampton's report of this battle. Gen. R. E. Lee, in his daily report to Richmond, said: "General Hampton, with his division, attacked the enemy's cavalry near Haw's Shop and drove them back on their infantry."

In conversation with Gen. Thomas L. Rosser in 1879, he made the following statement: "We had a strong position and could have held it until now, but "Rooney" Lee (Gen. W. H. F. Lee) reported that the infantry was coming up on his flank and he could not hold his position longer, and the whole line was, therefore, ordered to withdraw. One of Butler's officers refused to obey the order to retreat. I remonstrated with him until a shot passed between us, cutting his sword knot, when I told him if he was fool enough to stay there, he might do so, and left him." This accounts for Captain Pinckney's capture with about thirty prisoners. General Rosser said the officer apologized the next day, saying he thought he should obey only Hampton. A reliable neighbor, a guide to Gen. W. H. F. Lee , confirmed the statement, saying he saw the infantry advancing on Hampton's Brigade. Instead of a great a victory for the Federals, as they claim, the Confederates held them back a whole day. The whole Army of the Potomac halted and formed a line of battle in rear of the cavalry while General Lee was getting his army in line and fortifying over two miles in Hampton's rear. One of the Yankee reports says the Confederates left 180 dead on the field. This is not so. When the citizens of the neighborhoods gathered up the Confederate dead, they found only twenty-four killed in this battle and two killed on the 3rd of June, right at Haw's Shop. These they buried in Enon Churchyard, a mile below. The Yankees held the battle field and buried their dead around Enon Church, which was between the line of battle, cutting their names on sides and back of the church and putting temporary markers over other graves. After the war they were gathered up and buried in national cemeteries. The Confederate dead they placed in shallow graves, (five South Carolinians in a washout) throwing a little dirt on them. After the war several parties came on from South Carolina to get the bodies of their dead, but only one party was able to identify the remains sufficiently to remove them. In 1866, Judge Robinson, of Columbia, wrote to General Logan, who in turn wrote to our family, to ascertain if it were possible to find the remains of his son. On inquiry of a neighbor whose house was between the lines of battle, we learned that they had seen a soldier's foot protruding from a shallow grave, with the name of Robinson marked on his underwear. These facts were written to the Judge, who came on to Virginia, bringing with him a young man who was in the same company with his son. This man said he could not identify the battle field, being so short time on it, but that four of them behind a pine tree, two next to the tree on either side and two behind, these firing at the Yankees who were close up in some small pines. That he saw a Yankee aiming at them and told Robinson, who was immediately in front of him, to look out. Hardly had the warning been given when a bullet crashed through Robinson's brain, also striking him on the head and knocking him insensible. And he showed a scar marking the path of the bullet from front to back on top of his head. When the body was taken up, we found the skull pierced through and through by a bullet, and found one gold filling in a back tooth. Not fully satisfied, the Judge returned home, but came back with his wife, who identified the body by the teeth and clothing.

As we have seen, the cause of Captain Pinckney's capture was due to a disobedience of orders through a misunderstanding. When Wickham's Brigade opened the fight, Lieutenant Christian led the advance guard, with his company mounted, and when near Enon Church the Yankees fired on them from behind a fence. Private St. George T. Brooke was shot in the thigh and left in the road. A Yankee put him in a fence corner and put a rail across to protect him from the tramping of the horses. He was carried to my father's yard with the Federal wounded. At the request of our family, when the Yankees carried their wounded to Salem Church, Brooke was left at the house. The next day Hancock's Corps passed up the road and the chief surgeon of the corps, Dr. Calhoun, of New York, camped for the night in the yard. When told of Brooke's condition, he extracted the bullet from his leg and made him as comfortable as possible. He returned the next day from the front, four miles, bringing with him a wire splint to support his leg. A chaplain in the same corps, the Rev. Mr. Twitchel, of Maine, also visited him, bringing some lemons, a very rare luxury at that time. The latter gentleman was an intimate college friend of Maj. Robert Stiles, C.S.A., at Yale. Brooke recovered, but was always lame. He was professor of law for years at the University of West Virginia, at Morgantown.

The Confederates had no entrenchments. I walked over the field repeatedly and never saw any. Near where Robinson was killed, a short, shallow ditch had been dug before the war, very narrow, and not more than one hundred feet long. This happened to be just on the Confederate line and was used as a rifle pit. The Yankees reported over two hundred and fifty wounded and eighty-five killed. We may safely put their loss at four hundred killed and wounded and missing. Our loss unknown; twenty-four dead buried in Enon churchyard, and some few carried entirely off the field are all that I can account for. My father's house was in a large oak grove, half a mile from the actual battle line. The Yankees placed a battery of horse artillery in the yard, and this drew the fire of the Confederate batteries. Many shells struck the trees in the grove and passed near the house, killing four horses in the yard, two near the yard, and forty on the farm. A shell struck a lieutenant, cutting his leg off and killing his horse, within fifty yards of the house. Shells passed through a storehouse and smokehouse in the rear of the dwelling.

In the beginning of the fight, the Federals used my father's kitchen, a large building in the yard, for a hospital. While operating, a shell struck the chimney, just above the roof, knocking out a cartload of bricks; and another entered the operating room and fell under the table, fortunately not exploding. The medical director of the Army of Potomac, in his report, says: "The medical officers of this hospital displayed great gallantry, as the building, at times, was under heavy fire, several shells striking the building, one falling under the operating table." The hospital was then moved down to Haw's Shop and Salem Church and the schoolhouse used for a hospital. My father's mother and one sister were in our dwelling while the battle was in progress. With some of the negro servants, they took refuge in the very shallow basement, while shells were passing on both sides and above the house. Only one struck it, cutting the corner board and passing through the covered way to the basement and through the back porch.

On the 3rd of June, after the infantry had been withdrawn from this part of the line to Cold Harbor and Wilson's Division of Cavalry had taken its place, another cavalry fight occurred at Haw's Shop. Hampton and Rosser charged through the yard, and a member of the family gave the letters she had written for Captain Pinckney and the thirty South Carolina prisoners to their friends to be mailed home.

On the morning of the fight, Chapman Tyler, a member of Garey's Brigade, whose father's farm was the scene of the hardest part of the battle, the house being between the lines, was acting as guide for Gen. Fitz Lee. While sitting on his horse near General Lee, a shell burst near a the staff, a piece striking him on the head, and he died in a few days, killed within a few rods of his childhood home.

The grave in Enon churchyard holding the remains of the twenty-six soldiers killed in the two battles of Haw's Shop is entirely neglected, no mark whatever to locate it. Most of them were South Carolinians. An association has been formed in Virginia to mark all of the battle fields in the State. They have already marked some, among them one at Enon Church (called Haw's Shop) and one at Haw's Shop.

IN THE BATTLE OF FIRST COLD HARBOR

By Joseph R. Haw
Hampton, Va.

Published in the *Confederate Veteran Magazine, Volume XXXVI, January 1926, No. 1*

I have read, with interest, "First Lessons in War," by I. G. Bradwell, in the Octobe*r Veteran*. His account of the part taken by his command in the battle of first Cold Harbor is no doubt correct, but when he undertakes to describe the battle and battle fields on the Confederate right, he is very much in error. He speaks of our men being decimated by the fire of the enemy in their chosen position behind "Powhite Creek" that the enemy occupied a hill on the east side of the creek and millpond (Gaines's Mill), made more difficult to cross by the trees cut to fall into them, and so for the Gaines's millpond and mill are a mile or more from the hill, or bluff, as some historians call it. The mill and pond are on the north side of the road leading from New Bridge over the Chickahominy Swamp to old Cold Harbor. The water, after flowing over the overspout wheel close to the road, crosses the road in a somewhat southeast direction, takes the name of Powhite, and flows through Gaines's farm, which is also called Powhite, and on to the Chickahominy swamp.

It runs about at a right angle to both battle lines forming the right terminus of the Confederate line and the Yankee left terminus. Longstreet's Corps passed over this road to reach Fitzjohn [Fitz-John] Porter's line of battle, which was formed behind a small stream called Boson [Boatswain] Swamp, on the Watt, Joe Adams, and McGhee farms. A Massachusetts regiment, bringing up the rear of Porter's army on its retreat from Mechanicsville and Beaver Dam, halted at the mill and delayed our troops for a short time while Porter was forming his line of battle. The plateau, and bluff occupied by the Yanks was a part of my grandmother Watt's farm, and Boson [Boatswain] Swamp formed one of the dividing lines between it and Gaines's farm, flowing in a slight curve around the foot of the bluff. When a boy, I waded in the stream and it was nowhere up to my knees. The position on the Confederate right was naturally very strong; underbrush, briers, and the deep banks of the stream were very formidable, but on the center and left the land was of a more gentle slope. I am confident that neither Boson [Boatswain] Swamp or Chickahominy were much swollen on the 27th of June, 1862, when this battle was fought. At the time, Seven Pines was fought, nearly a month previous, the Chickahominy was flooded, and McClellan's roads and bridges were very incomplete, but on the 27th both roads and bridges were in good condition, the road in rear of this position especially so. Nor do I think the Yanks were so badly demoralized as the writer thinks. Fitzjohn [Fitz-John] Porter fought this battle, and he also fought at the battle of Malvern Hill, which was certainly victory for the Yanks, as the Confederates were repulsed all along the line. Walter Harrison, Assistant Adjutant and Inspector General of Pickett's Division, in his book called "Pickett's Men," describes vividly the final capture of this position by Pickett's Brigade, supported by R. H. Anderson's Brigade of South Carolina. Harrison was in the charge and within ten paces of General Pickett when he was wounded. Comrade Bradwell says: "In this battle ground is a Federal Cemetery in which stands an urn which contains the remains, or parts, of eighteen thousand Yankee soldiers killed in this fight and the one which took place here June 2 and 3, 1864." The Cold Harbor National Cemetery contains bodies of Federal soldiers gathered from the two battles of Cold Harbor and other battles in the surrounding territory. I had visited this cemetery shortly after it was established, and had seen a large mound said to contain unknown dead, and was sure that a lot of the dead were buried under the sod. To refresh my memory, I visited Hampton National Cemetery and interviewed the keeper, who had recently been the keeper of Cold Harbor. He told me there were eight hundred and eighty-nine unknown buried in the mound, and a total of nineteen hundred and seventy-one in the cemetery. At my written request, the Quartermaster General, War Department, Washington, has sent me a full list of National Cemeteries in the United States and the number of interments in each, and this is the official report for Cold Harbor, Va.: "Area in acres, 1 3/4; unknown interred, 1,338; known, 633; total, 1,971." It may be of interest to know that there are interred in all National Cemeteries, from Louisiana to Alaska, 399,579 soldiers. Of this number about 10,000 are Confederates. This report is for quarter ending March 31, 1925. No doubt many of these have been buried from Soldiers' Homes and other places since the War between the States.

"Grandmother"
Sarah Bohannon Kidd Watt
b. 15 Dec 1784, d. 22 Apr 1863,
Wife of Hugh Watt, Mother of George Watt

Story and Incident
for the *Christian Observer*

My Visits to Grandmother

By M. J. Haw

(This is not a fancy sketch, but a literal record of experiences amid scenes and events of historic interest.)

When I was ten years old [1845], there were seven of us, my sister [Sarah Eliza] older than myself and five younger brothers [John Hugh, George Pitman, William, Edwin and Joseph Richardson]. Ours was a quiet, country neighborhood [Haw's Shop/Studley], where there were few diversions for the young; besides, our careful mother [Mary Austin Watt Haw, wife of John Haw, III] thought home the best place for children, so our annual visit to grandmother [Sarah Bohannon Kidd Watt at Springfield Farm] was the great event of the year. For months beforehand it was the subject of delightful anticipations, and for months afterwards the subject of fond and pleasing reminiscences. When the bustle of preparation was over, and the cavalcade was ready to start, we quivered with excitement and were wild with joy. The carriage, containing mother, sister, myself, the baby and the next youngest boy, led the procession. Next followed a farm cart with the nurse, the third youngest boy and the trunks. The two older boys, riding horseback one behind the other, brought up the rear.

The month was August, when in ordinary seasons abundant rains have freshened the grass and foliage parched by the July heat, and started the roses on their second profuse blooming; when the fields of Indian corn are in their richest luxuriance, the vineyards and orchards bending under the choicest fruits, and luscious melons, green and golden, gleaming among the luxuriant vines that cover many acres.

The distance was ten miles, and the road wound alternately through a level or gently rolling country, sometimes along shady lanes bordered by rail-fences overrun with the graceful Virginia creeper, the gorgeous trumpet vine, and wild grape and sloe vines. Then it would pass through sunny spaces amid cornfields and orchards; and anon it would plunge us into the dim, cool shade of a dense wood. Frequently it led across limpid brooks, rippling over their pebbly beds and bordered up to the roadway with ferns, wild iris, and feathery grasses. At one point, it led by a rustic bridge over the dark, slowly flowing waters of Totopotomoy Creek, into which the willows, beeches, and cork-elms dipped their pendent branches.

Eagerly we looked out for each familiar landmark, and wondered that the long period of a year had not produced greater changes. But pleasant as was the journey, we did not for a moment forget the goal, and when we turned off from the highway into a private road, which led through a strip of woods and an open field to the house a quarter of a mile away, we fairly shouted with delight.

As we came in sight, how cosy and home-like the old square, gray farmhouse looked embowered in venerable locusts, at whose feet spread a smooth, green turf, on which no leaf nor twig was allowed to rest. The althea hedge, which screened the kitchen from the back yard, was in full bloom; and the hedge of Scotch roses bordering the opposite end of the yard, was full of pale pink, waxlike blossoms. As we passed the orchard on our right, the breeze wafted to us the fragrance of ripe apples and peaches.

Some little negroes were watching for our arrival; and as soon as they ran to the house with the tidings, grandmother came out, looking so trim and immaculate in her neat gingham dress and snowy cap. What a kissing and hugging there was, as we all clung around her! Then came the cook and the housemaids to shake hands and delight us by exclaiming how pretty we were and how much we had grown; while a gang of little darkeys in the rear, stood staring and grinning and bobbing their woolly heads.

As soon as the greetings were over, we scampered away to explore every nook and corner and see if everything was where it had always been and as it had always been. We never found any change, nor had there been, I dare say, for forty years. One of the first places to be visited was a brick-floored basement room, where we always found a row of long, smooth, dark green Jackson water-melons flanked by piles of greenish yellow musk-melons -- cantaloupes had not then come in fashion. Another object of interest was the old-fashioned corner-cupboard, where were displayed the blue and white dinner set of the Chinese willow pattern, the dainty gilt-bordered tea set, and on the top shelf a collection of toy mugs and pitchers once the property of our little Aunt Sarah [Eliza Watt, 1825-1830], the family pet and darling, who, at the tender age of five years, had died thirty years ago. With tender reverence we would gaze at these, and handle them with loving care when permitted to do so. We never tired of hearing about this little girl, whose memory was so tenderly cherished; and whenever we saw grandmother unlock her "chest of drawers," (old name for bureau) we would beg her to show us Aunt Sarah's little white dresses, dimity petticoats, tiny red slippers and the yellow curl cut from her little head as she lay in her coffin.

At noon the cook would blow the horn to call Uncle Peter [Pitman Kidd Watt] and the hands from the field; and soon after this, dinner would be served. Such ham, such chicken, such cornfield peas and sweet potatoes, I have never tasted since. Soon after dinner the servants would pile armfuls of melons under a table standing beneath a big tree in the back yard; and Uncle Peter, brandishing the carving knife, would cry out, "Who wants some water-melon? Green rind, red meat, full of juice and so sweet." Quickly under his practiced stroke, the crisp melon, cracking before the advancing knife, would be splint in two, a tablespoon stuck in each half and the company served, the elders standing around the table to enjoy the feast and the children sitting upon the grass. Ah! that was happiness.

In the early mornings and late afternoons, followed by a retinue of little negroes, we would explore the surrounding fields and, except at one point, where the land, jutting out into the valley, rose considerably above the plateau, forming what we considered an imposing elevation. From the wild pea-vines with which it was covered when not in cultivation, it was called The Pea Mount. As it commanded an extensive view, and moreover was crowned with a group of seedling peach trees whose fruit we considered very fine, we often visited this spot.

Another favorite walk was to Parsons Spring. The water of the Gum Spring at the foot of the garden not being very cold, the drinking water was brought from a better spring on the opposite side of the plantation. The path to this spring led through the peach orchard, down a wooded hill, across a pebbly brook and up another wooded hill. On the side of this hill, densely shaded by beech and laurel, lined with green moss and fringed with ferns and grasses, was Parson's Spring, its ice-cold water so clear that every pebble on its glistening, white bottom was plainly visible. On our journeys to this spring, we often amused ourselves playing "Snake in the Gully," running up and down the hills and leaping the brook in trying to elude the pursuing snake. Alas! in our innocent sport, when our glad voices and merry laughter were ringing through the wood, how little we dreamed what a fearful game would one day be played on that quiet spot, armed men rushing in deadly combat across the ravine, the roar of cannon shaking the hills, and the rivulet running blood.

.   .   .

As the years rolled on, we continued to visit grandmother, not the whole family in a body, but in detachments. But although we loved her dearly and enjoyed the comforts of her well ordered home, our visits were not the occasion of such ecstatic delight as in our younger days; for it was so lonesome there, so very lonesome.

The house was shut off by a body of woods from the public highway, and there was no signs of a human habitation visible except one house. Grandmother's disposition and habits were very domestic. She had always been a busy woman and a notable housekeeper, and, therefore, had never visited or entertained a great deal. Now many of her old friends were dead, and some were too decrepit to get about well. Their children were all married and gone away, and their grandchildren rarely visited them; so there were no young people with whom we could exchange visits.

Grandmother was old, and Uncle Peter, in disposition and ways, was still older. In her youth books and newspapers had been so rare that she had not formed the habit of reading; and the sayings and doings of his neighbors supplied all the mental pabulum craved by the intellect of Uncle Peter, to whom the world did not exist beyond a radius of ten miles; so the family library was scant. So dull and monotonous was existence there that we dubbed it "the off corner of the world, the jumping off place," and vowed that the most daring and indefatigable explorer would never be able to find it. Little we thought that in a few years the eyes of the world would be fixed upon that quiet, remote spot, and that the name of the Watt Farm would go down in history.

One visit to grandmother stands out prominently in memory, when she invited her five elder granddaughters, ranging in age from sixteen to eighteen years, to a protracted quilting party. As was the custom in that primitive day, she had made a bed quilt for each of her children. Uncle Peter's she had quilted herself with the aid of her handmaidens. Those for her two daughters [Mary Austin and Margaret Mills] she had merely pieced together and left to be quilted by them. It was to quilt those for her two younger sons [Hugh Washington and George] that we were invited to visit her.

The job of quilting was not very enticing to us, for we were rather lazy in our young days. I dare say if we had known how much hard work was before us in the dreadful years to come, we would have been even lazier than we were. But we wished to gratify grandmother; besides, it would be quite a frolic for all of us to be together, and we knew there would be melons and fruit galore and all sorts of good eating.

When Uncle Peter's quilt was brought out for our inspection and imitation, we were dismayed at the narrow rows of the quilting and the almost invisible stitches. But our consternation soon gave way to interest and curiosity as grandmother proceeded to point out bits of chintz and gingham like dresses our mothers had worn in their childhood. We greatly admired the fine texture and dainty patterns of these goods, which were evidently imported, and wondered at the high prices, none less than fifty cents a yard. But a keener interest was excited in examining pieces of domestic gingham, "Virginia cloth," of pretty colors and as fine in texture as the ginghams that sell now at eight cents a yard. Among these, was a lustrous piece of white and yellow plaid with a queer name and made of a mixture of cotton and raw silk, both grown on the plantation of my great-great-grandfather [John Austin]. In the center of the quilt, grandmother pointed out, as the gem of the collection, two pieces of calico, one like a dress of her mother's and the other like a dress of her grandmother's [Mary Crenshaw Austin]. The first had been manufactured on the plantation of her grandfather [John Austin], Bosworth on the Chickahominy. From cotton raised on the place, the seeds had been picked out by hand, the fiber carded, spun, and woven by hand, the fabric bleached, and then sent to England to be stamped. After twice crossing the ocean in a sailing vessel, it had been made up into short-waisted, narrow-skirted, big-sleeved dresses for Mrs. John Austin's daughters [Susanna, Elizabeth, Sarah and Mary]. At the same time that this goods had been stamped, Mrs. Austin had caused to be purchased for herself in England a calico dress at the cost of seven shillings (nearly $1.75) a yard; and a piece of this costly calico was now occupying a place of honor in Uncle Peter's bedquilt.

"By the bye," said grandmother, "one of the women who helped to spin this dress of my mother's is living now, and is nearly a hundred years old. I must take you to see 'Aunt' Phyllis."

"Who is 'Aunt' Phyllis?" we asked.

"She was one of grandfather's people, and at his death she fell to one of his daughters, who married a Quaker. He set all of his wife's negroes free, and "Aunt" Phyllis had to make her own living. As she was an uncommonly smart and industrious negro, she got on right well until she became too old to work. Then one of my nephews, who owned several of her children, took her to his home to live with her daughter. Not long ago, his wife died, his home was broken up, and his negroes scattered.

When I was a child living at grandfather's after mother's death, "Aunt" Phyllis was so good and kind to me that I always loved her; so when I heard she was homeless, I had a room built onto Sybelia's quarter and moved her here. Sybelia's girl, Lucy, stays with her and waits on her, and I send her meals from the table and go every day to see if she is comfortable. It is wonderful how she has retained her senses and her faculties so long. She is so grateful that it is a pleasure to do for her; and I enjoy talking with her about the life at grandfather's, and the old people we knew, now dead and gone. She is very religious, and delights in hearing me read the Bible Sunday evenings and singing with me some old hymns that she remembers perfectly and sings in a remarkable clear, sweet voice. You must be sure to go to see 'Aunt' Phyllis."

Of course we went to see "Aunt" Phyllis. Grandmother would have been displeased had we not gone; besides, we had never seen a centenarian. And having gone once, we went many times; for her memory was excellent, and we were greatly interested in her stories of the olden times and of our dead and gone ancestors. She retained a vivid recollection of the Revolutionary War, especially of the terror excited by Tarleton's passage through the county [June, 1781] on his way to join Cornwallis at Yorktown. And she described how her master had sent away wagons loaded with provisions, the young negro men, and the best horses to his farm in Cumberland, and how her mistress had her silk dresses, her silver-ware and her best china buried among the fig bushes in the corner of the garden. And she explained that the blur in the middle of the gilt-framed mirror in grandmother's sitting room, was caused by the glass having been buried at that time. Their fears of British atrocities, however, were not realized, as they saw nothing of the enemy but the red-coats dashing about the lower fields, chasing and driving off cattle and horses.

The quilting proceeded leisurely. Frequently, one or two of us, or all in a body, would adjourn with plates and knives to the peach orchard temptingly in sight, or to the table under the tree, where melons might be served at any hour desired. And sometimes we would sit on the grass in the back yard among the group of sable aunties peeling apples to dry, and, while eating the mellow apples they would obligingly peel and offer us, encourage them to talk of the childhood of our parents, of the "hants" that frequented the graveyard, and of their religious experiences.

In the late afternoon we would climb the Pea Mount to view the sunset, or stroll through the woods around Parsons Spring gathering ferns and wild flowers. Sometimes, when feeling unusually energetic, we would cross the low grounds to the Chickahominy, nearly half a mile away, and wander along the banks of that dark, sluggish stream gathering mussel shell and stone arrow-heads for mementoes. Through the twilight gloom shed by the dense foliage over the scene, the gnarled trunks of the trees and their twisted roots denuded by frequent overflows, assumed such fantastic shapes that we could almost imagine we saw Indians gliding among them, or peering at us from behind some hoary beech or birch.

At last, after several weeks thus spent, the quilting party ended. Our grandmother praised our work, thanked us warmly, and presented to each of us a five dollar gold piece as a reward for our industry.

. . .

In the spring of 1862, I made my last visit to grandmother. It was a sad and gloomy time. For a year the country had been writhing in the throes of a cruel war. Fathers, husbands, and brothers were gathered in distant camps; bloody battles had been fought; thousands had been slain and other thousands maimed for life. But so far we had escaped the ravages of war, and we fondly hoped to remain undisturbed.

Our dream of fancied security was rudely broken by the report that [Gen. George B.] McClellan's army was advancing up the Peninsula and the Confederate army falling back before it, which would bring one or the other army upon us.

For several weeks, grandmother, now seventy-eight years old, had been seriously ill, and mother had been at her bedside. One day mother unexpectedly returned, and shocked us with the tidings that the Confederate army, now rapidly approaching, would take a position in defense of Richmond on the other side of the Chickahominy, leaving our whole section in the Federal lines. As grandmother's condition was somewhat improved, and mother was unwilling to be parted from her young family in such trying circumstances, she had left the invalid for a day in the care of her faithful and devoted maid and nurse, and of an old friend who had been helping to nurse her, intending to send me back in the carriage to fill the position of housekeeper and head nurse.

When I arrived near night-fall, everything was so quiet and unchanged that I could scarcely believe we were on the verge of such terrible experiences. But as soon as it grew dark, we could plainly see the glow of the Confederate camp fires on the hills beyond the Chickahominy. And a negro returning from Richmond brought messages from my three brothers, whose regiment, the Fifteenth Virginia Infantry, was occupying the most advanced position opposite to us.

Soon after my arrival, my grandmother rallied and seemed so much stronger, that the friend who had been assisting in nursing her returned to her home to look after her own family.

Several days of anxiety and suspense followed. Uncle Peter rode out daily to hear the news and watch the passing of the Confederate army.

Then he reported that he had seen the rear-guard pass out of sight, and that by the morning the enemy would be upon us.

About ten o'clock the next morning, we saw a squadron of cavalry pass through the place, and a little later, some stragglers from an infantry camp near by, came into the yard. They politely requested us to sell them milk, butter and eggs, but did not attempt to enter the house or to disturb anything outside. Nor were they noisy or disagreeable. Our own soldiers could not have behaved better. We did not realize until two years later, how blessed we were in having as commander of this invading army a Christian gentleman [Gen. Fitz-John Porter], who maintained perfect discipline in his army and strictly observed the rules of civilized warfare.

Still, how harrowing was the situation. At night I watched the light of my brothers' camp fires, and by day trembled as the house rocked with the roar of cannon throwing shot and shell into their camp. There was frequent skirmishing, daily cannonading, and hourly expectation of a terrible battle.

The season advanced, the turf was like emerald, the roses bloomed, and the old locusts, with their small, pale green leaves and showers of snowy blossoms, looked like huge bouquets. As I looked out upon the dewy freshness of a bright May morning, or at midnight gazed upon the still landscape bathed in the white moonbeams, the beauty which had heretofore delighted me, seemed to mock the anguish of my spirit.

Grandmother's great age and the extreme weakness of serious illness had so benumbed her faculties that she was incapable of fully comprehending the surrounding conditions; and, fortunately, she slept a great deal. In previous periods of convalescence, she had been accustomed to tempting her appetite with favorite delicacies, which she now craved and for which she would beg piteously. It was hard to make her understand why she could not have them; and sometimes she would seem deeply wounded by my apparent indifference and hard-heartedness, which sorely grieved me.

She had one of her hungry spells while the battle of Seven Pines [May 31, 1862] was raging, and the house was shaking from the roaring of musketry and the booming of cannon. As with an aching heart I was watching the smoke of battle rise over the trees beyond the Chickahominy, the Federal soldiers constructing a pontoon bridge across the swollen stream, the long, blue column wading through the flooded low grounds to pass over it, and the green branches of trees cut off by cannon balls breaking the glassy surface of the water, she was begging and fretting for something wholly unattainable.

McClellan did not permit his soldiers to steal, so the cattle and poultry being left us, we had milk, eggs and chicken soup with which to nourish her; and, in spite of the unfavorable surroundings, she slowly strengthened. Most fortunately, too, the negroes remained faithful. Although persuaded and entreated, and lured by specious stories and golden promises to leave, not one of them left or showed the slightest sign of insubordination.

On the afternoon of June 27, instead of the slow booming of cannon usual at that hour, we heard in the direction of Richmond rapid artillery firing and the rattling roar of musketry. Couriers dashing about, activity in the camp, and officers in groups talking excitedly, indicated that something unusual was going on. The noise of conflict continued and seemed to grow louder and nearer. Could this be the long expected battle? To our eager inquiries, an officer replied that the rebels had attacked McClellan's right wing. The battle which was to decide the fate of Richmond had begun. A miserable, sleepless night followed.

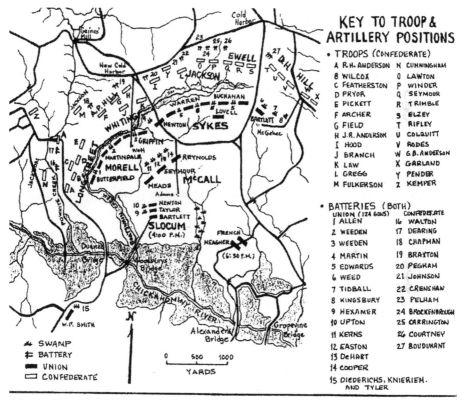

BATTLE OF GAINES' MILL - JUNE 27, 1862

Military Operations in Hanover County, Virginia, 1861-1865 by John M. Gabbert, p. 40.

In the early morning, cannonading was begun. All around us was bustle and commotion, infantry marching, cavalry dashing about, artillery and ammunition wagons rumbling through the fields. Cannon balls began to plow holes in the lower fields. Then one tore through the roof of the stable, and another knocked off the top of the kitchen chimney. The negroes ran from the outlying quarters to the dwelling house for protection. "Aunt" Betsy, the cook, rushed into the yard and cried wildly, "Whar is Mars Peter? Somebody go find Mars Peter. Ef they don't stop this foolishness, somebody is gwine to git hurt presently."

A Federal officer found Uncle Peter and told him that the Union army was falling back to this position, where they would make a stand, and that he must remove the family at once. Grandmother at first flatly refused to leave her home, but yielded to our entreaties on the condition that Uncle Peter would remain to take care of the house and the negroes. So Uncle Peter stayed (a little while) to take care of things as did the old man at Waterloo, of whom Victor Hugo tells in his graphic description of that famous battle. Thus does history repeat itself.

While the negro men were harnessing the horses to the carriage and a mule to a farm cart, the maid, "Jane", and I thrust some clothing and valuables into a trunk, which was taken to the cart. Two negro men bore their mistress tenderly to the carriage, where a bed had been arranged for her. I crept in beside her, "Jane" mounted the box with the driver, and we drove off. Thus grandmother left for the last time the home where she had reigned as mistress for sixty years.

For some distance we drove along the rear of the Federal line of battle, passing regiment after regiment drawn up in battle array. Then we turned to the right and drove as speedily as we could along the encumbered road to the rear. About three miles from the battlefield, we stopped at the house of a friend beyond Cold Harbor. It was a perilous journey. Sometimes a bomb would go shrieking over our heads or a cannon shot cut off a branch from a tree close beside us.

We were not the only refugees. Forty others, driven from their homes by the tide of battle, had taken refuge there before us; and in that wretched company, there was not one who did not have some near relative or dear friend fighting with Lee that day. The smoke of battle hung a "sulphurous canopy" over the woods bounding the horizon, and the roar of the guns was deafening. Separately or in groups, we sat about the yards or on the porches, with bowed heads and tearful eyes, engaged in silent prayer for the safety of our loved ones, the success of our cause.

Early the next morning, some passing Confederate cavalry brought the news that the Union army had been defeated and was retreating across the Chickahominy. That afternoon my uncle [George Watt], who lived in Richmond and had been searching all day for his mother, brought the welcome news that my brothers were unhurt. Grandmother's home, he said, had been the scene of the fiercest fighting of the day, and was a total wreck. It was now being used as a hospital, and every building on the place was crowded with the enemy's wounded.

•　　•　　•

Once more I visited my grandmother's former home. It was September, two months after the battle. As we emerged from the wood into the open, what a scene of desolation! There was not a trace of any enclosures, and where had been green fields of waving corn and dun meadows dotted with haystacks, was a wide expanse of weeds dotted with patches of yellow clay. As we drew nearer, a sickening odor pervaded the air.

The Confederates, wearied with marching and fighting, toiling under the heat of a June sun, and hurrying to follow up the retreating enemy, had given slight burial to either friend or foe. Many open graves from which their own dead had been removed, were not more than two feet deep; and upon the corpses of the enemy, they had simply thrown up mounds of earth. Everywhere were dead horses dried away in their skins like mummies.

What profound stillness and mournful silence brooded over the scene! In the tall weeds, the bushes and trees, there was not a twitter nor the flutter of a wing. For it is a well known fact that the sulphurous smoke and the noise of the guns drive every bird far away from the battlefield.

As we wandered over the fields, we found graves everywhere. From some of these, the rain had washed away much of the earth, disclosing grinning skulls and protruding hands upon which the skin had dried away like a shriveled glove. Into others wild animals had burrowed, scattering the bones around. Through a tangle of wild pea vines, we climbed the Pea Mount, where a battery had been placed to rake the valley over which the Confederates had to advance. On its crest were several dead horses, and around its base and sides many graves.

We strolled through the orchard s and along the woods bordering them, through which led the path to Parson's Spring. Here had been the fiercest fighting of the day, when [Gen. John Bell] Hood's Texans charged down one hill, across the brook, up another hill, and over a barricade of bales of hay and the branches of trees, driving the enemy before them. Where the peach orchard joined the apple orchard, a battery had been posted; and here were four dead horses lying almost in a heap. Along this line, in the shade of the trees and among the weeds and wild flowers, were not only single graves but trenches of the dead.

Last of all we visited the house. Rank weeds had sprung up even to the doors, except where the yellow clay glared in the sunlight. Even in the corners of the yard there were graves and bordering it was a long trench. In the garden was another trench said to contain forty dead.

The house, what a wreck! The walls and roof were torn by shot and shell, the weather-boarding honeycombed by minnie balls, and every pane of glass shattered. And the floors! -- grandmother's immaculate floors! In the summer they had always been kept bare, and the first sound heard in the morning would be a maid plying the dry-rubbing brush in the hall, while at almost any hour in the day, a couple of half grown girls might have been seen on their knees with an old slipper and a cracker plate of fine white sand rubbing up spots invisible to any eye but grandmother's. Now, from garret to cellar there was scarcely a space of flooring as large as a man's hand that did not bear the dark purple stain of blood.

What a harrowing spectacle this, of a once neat and comfortable home now a tenantless, foul and battered wreck -- the household furnishings accumulated and carefully preserved through many years -- the comforts of the living and the cherished mementos of the dead, all scattered and destroyed! I thought of Aunt Sarah's little white dresses, and dimity petticoats torn up to bandage bloody wounds -- and the little red slippers and golden curl, what had been their fate?

"Studley"

The birthplace of Patrick Henry.

Written by Miss M. J. Haw, and copied very carefully from her "Scrapbook"by her niece Nannie B. Haw, on Nov. 13, 1939. This was written apparently Oct. 15, 1881.

The recent Centennial commemorations of the various events of the Revolution which converted the thirteen British colonies of America into the greatest republic the world has beheld, have directed public attention with an engrossing interest to the characters-as well as the occurrences, of that stirring period. Among the former there is perhaps not another more striking and unique than, the great American orator, whose bold spirit and impassioned utterances were so largely instrumental in inciting his countrymen to the successful resistance [sic] of British injustice. A recent visit to the birthplace of this eminent Virginian has suggested the thought that a sketch of it might possess some interest for the public.

"Studley," where on the 29th of May, 1736, Patrick Henry was born, is in the lower part of Hanover County, Virginia, and distant about sixteen miles from Richmond and eight miles from Hanover courthouse, at which latter place, it will be remembered, Henry made his first public speech, electrifying his countrymen by an eloquence till then unimagined among them. This section, lying between, the Chickahominy and James rivers is the upper part of what is known as the "Peninsula", has no natural feature of striking beauty or interest. It is level but slightly undulating, and is intersected by numerous brooks and small creeks. Much of the county is covered by forests of oak, hickory, pine, cedar, gum, beech, and various other trees. The soil is poor, with the exception of that lying along the rivers and creeks and the principal crops grown are corn, wheat, oats, potatoes, melons, etc.

The original "Sturley"[sic] plantation contained six or seven hundred acres of land, and was bounded on the south by Totopotomoy Creek and on the north by a road leading from Richmond to Hanover Town, a colonial mart, and once a place of such importance that it was near being the capital of the State; now simply a ferry on the Pamunkey River, with nothing to mark the former site of crowded warehouses and busy streets but the log hut of the ferrymen.

"Studley" ceased to be the residence of Patrick Henry during his early childhood, his father at that time removing to a plantation on the Pamunkey river [South Anna] known as "Retreat" [Mt. Brilliant was the original home on the plantation.]. It then became the property of Judge Peter Lyons of the

91

State Supreme Court of Appeals, and was for many years his residence. But for some time after it continued to be the burial place of the Henry family and until quite recently the brick wall enclosing the graves of Patrick Henry's father [buried at Mt. Brilliant] and other members of the family [probably also buried at Mt. Brilliant] was still standing. [No wall stands today, only marked grave is that of Dr. Thomas Chrystie.]. Judge Lyons was a gentleman of wealth and taste and did much to preserve and beautify the place. During his life it was the cherished home of a happy family and the seat of a generous and elegant hospitality.

Forty years ago it was a fine example of the Virginia Plantation of that day. Of moderate fertility, it was yet cultivated by a numerous slave population, whose cabins, grouped here and there, each with its little garden, henhouse and pigpen, added greatly to the cheerfulness of the scene. The old Henry house had been destroyed by fire, but at what period is unknown. The Lyons residence was a capacious wooden building with a wide airy hall, pleasant chambers, and shady porches. This was surrounded by a large yard ornamented with fine shade trees and rare shrubs, and a wide smooth lawn sloping away to the south. Leading in opposite direction from this lawn to the two gates by which the plantation was entered was a broad avenue, formed by double rows on each side of aspens catalpa, and other handsome shade trees. On the north of the house, bordering the yard lay and [sic] endearing old-fashioned garden, such as the English delight in, where fragrant flowers, luscious fruits, medicinal herbs, and kitchen vegetables were mingled in charming proximity and profusion,. Broad, straight graveled walks, bordered with roses and flowering shrubs, led in four directions to a large, square summer-house in the center, over-run with jasmine and honeysuckle. A serpentine walk, bordered with boxwood, led doen [sic]) one side to a vine-clad aebor [sic] at one end of the garden, and rustic seats in many a nook invited one to repose.

In the present mania for the antique, what a treasury would be that old house, with its queer wall-papering, where shepherds and shepherdesses, with broad hat and orthodox crook, tended their flocks on mossy banks, and with the family portraits in heavy gilt or oaken frames, where smiling dames in low bodices and towering hair secured with ample combs, and stately gentlemen in ruffled shirts, rich vestments, and powdered wigs looked down upon the fine old, quaintly-carved mahogany furniture, and the glossy waxed floors!

At that time "Studley" was the property of Judge Lyons' youngest daughter, a wealthy widow, who usually spent the winter in Richmond and much of the summer in traveling, so that it was only at intervals that the old family residence, was occupied. But during her absence a skilled overseer and trained servants carried on the farming operations and the domestic machinery as faithfully and efficiently as if under the eye of the mistress. Regularly was the lawn mown, the box hedges trimmed, and the yard kept clear of weeds and fallen leaves. A diligent gardener tilled the garden and gathered the seeds and herbs in their season. Dusky maids daily aired the chambers, "dry-rubbed" the floors, and polished the furniture. At any season or any hour that the mistress might come, all that was necessary to be done for her entertainment was to light the fire and cook the meals. And such visits were gala seasons for the negroes and the neighbors, who delighted to see something of the wonted old life and animation about the place.

Such was the "Studley" of forty years ago as remembered by old residents in its vicinity; but the "Studley" of today how changed! Its owner, Mrs. Richardson, married a second time, and dying not many years later, bequeathed her property to her husband. This gentleman was an alien to the State, and being a stranger to the family into which he had married was indifferent to its traditions and associations. Thoroughly utilitarian in his views, he laid vandal hands upon the fine old place. The house was pulled down, and with a portion of the materials a smaller one was built upon a distant part of the estate. In this a new overseer was installed, with orders to cut down the trees of the yard and avenue, grub up the flowers and shrubs, plow over yard, garden and lawn, and plant the whole in corn. With heavy hearts and woeful countenances the faithful slaves performed the bitter task; and piteous were the lamentations they poured into the ears of the sympathizing neighbors. The work of spoiliation was so complete that now a single magnolia tree alone marks the site of the old house, and in the spring some scattered jonquils and crocuses give evidence of where once the garden lay.

This vandalism failed to enrich the perpetrator, who a few years later died a bankrupt. "Studley" was then put upon the market, and the faithful slaves, noted for their intelligence and good character, were by sale scattered far and near.

In common with the surrounding country, this place has felt the blight of war, and a yet more appalling blight in the social and financial upheaval consequent - a revolution, indeed, such as has seldom shaken the foundations of any state. Nearly twenty years ago "Studley" was sold again, and in two portions.

On the northern part, which contains the graveyards of the Henry and Lyons families and the site of the Lyons residence, stands a neat and comfortable farmhouse; and in the surrounding fields are grown the crops common to the section.

The southern part is devoted to what is commonly called "truck farming" that is, the raising of vegetables and melons for the Richmond market. The farmer's residence consists of a cluster of little log-cabin with potatoes and cornfield peas growing up to the doorsteps. That the birthplace of

Henry will ever produce another such genius is scarcely within the range of possibility

M.J.H

PART THREE

THE HOMES

HOMES

Often we find ourselves looking at articles, census details and family histories as separate, standalone entities as we research our ancestors. It is important to be able to see a larger picture — to put people in a physical place. What evokes the spirit of these people more than images and history of their homes?

Most of the homes mentioned in the preceeding articles by Dr. T. W. Hooper, Joseph Richard Haw, and M. J. Haw, are provided in this section to help provide a richer context for their memories. Although some have been lost, many of the homes are still standing.

The history of these homes was researched by the Hanover County Historical Society and published in *Old Homes of Hanover County, Virginia* in 1983. Two homes, Locust Hill and the Kidd House, were not part of the original book but have been added for this work.

With the permission of the Hanover County Historical Society, the relevant material is reprinted here. (Note: References to "current" ownership refer to the time of publication in 1983.)

These mini-histories provide a clearer insight into Dr. Hooper's, and the Haws' articles. They serve to tie the families together and in time and place.

Where possible in this publications the photograph that illustrated articles in the original book have been exchanged for drawings by various artists taken from the Pamunkey Woman's Club calendars with their kind permission..

Avondale (circa 1820). *Pamunkey Woman's Club Calendar,* January 1990, by Janet Ogden Thompson.

Avondale

Avondale is located on Route 606 on the edge of the subdivision bearing the same name, a contrast between its architecture and that of its twentieth century neighbors. Avondale was built about 1820, according to tradition, by Thomas Gardner (ca. 1799-1858). He married Sarah Hendron Meredith (1806-1845) of Craney Island. Thomas Gardner's father, Reuben Gardner, gave him the land and confirmed the gift in his will which was proved in 1843. It is believed that Avondale was built by the same person who built Totomoi, which is located nearby, as there are some architectural similarities between the two houses. In the 1850 U. S. census, Thomas Gardner had real estate valued at $11,000.

The central portion of the house has two large rooms in an English basement, two rooms and a large hall on the first floor and three rooms and a hall on the second floor. The stairway, which ascends from the hall, is notable for the scrolled-work under the stair ends. Two large exterior chimneys on the west end of the house serve five fireplaces. The floor plan, the interior trim, and the method of construction place Avondale within the Federal style of American architecture. In 1835 Thomas Gardner made a three-room addition on the west side, one room in the basement and one room on each of the two levels above. Writing found on a piece of siding from the addition indicates that Mr. Wingfield built the addition in that year.

During the Civil War, Avondale figured prominently in the actions leading to the Battle of Cold Harbor. In May 1864 General Lee and General Grant faced each other along Totopotomoy Creek as they moved from positions on the North Anna River to Cold Harbor. Confederate General John C. Breckinridge established temporary headquarters at Avondale while he faced Union General Wingfield Scott Hancock. Although there was no general engagement along Totopotomoy Creek, Avondale bears witness to the intensity of the skirmishing that transpired as Confederate and Union troops attempted to find weaknesses in the others line. The frame-work of the house is riddled with small shot. Marks on the mantel in the north room on the first floor show where small shot was embedded and the path of one bullet that entered a north window, nicked the door, and embedded itself in the surround of a south window, can still be traced.

Avondale has had several owners since the Civil War: the Merediths,Timberlakes, Borkeys, Rhinesmiths, Pollack, Easter, and now belongs to the Charles M. Bourne family.

Beaverdam. *Pamunkey Woman's Club Calendar,* July 1995, by Carol A. Bock.

Beaverdam [Beaver Dam]

This Beaverdam home is located on Cold Harbor Road in Mechanicsville and is not to be confused with another Beaverdam in the upper section of the county, the home of the Fontaine family. In 1787 the name of Col. William White appears on the tax list for the first time with 283 acres. By 1813 Capt. William White's name is shown with 334 acres "called Beverdam [sic]" which adjoined William Austin (Walnut Lane) on the Chickahominy Swamp. William White was dead by 1821 when "estate" is shown and in 1827 the property was divided between his heirs: Mildred White, William S. White, Philip B. White, Thomas J. White, and Elizabeth White. In 1836, Joseph Hooper purchased 93-1/4 acres from Thomas J. White and others adjoining William Austin. By 1854 Joseph Hooper had died and his estate sold the property to Charles Pollard. Five years later, William Catlin was the owner. He died in 1882 survived by his third wife, Rebecca R. Catlin, who sold to Edward A. Catlin in 1893 all her interest in tract of land called Beaver Dam 140 acres. The next owners were John and Robert Carter.

From the files of the Mutual Assurance Society of Virginia, there is an insurance policy on Beaver Dam. The dwelling house was insured for $1,200 in 1801. Apparently the house was built by Capt. William White who was living there at that time, but the exact date is unknown. The sketch shows two houses joined by a breezeway.

Beaverdam stands on historic soil. It was the site on which was fought the first of the series of battles around Richmond. The stream, bearing the same name, and which flows through the farm, was said to run red with blood after the battle. In the article by Dr. Thomas W. Hooper (*Richmond Dispatch*, February 3, 1895), he stated, "The last time I stood under the roof was a few days after the battle and all around me were unburied dead, while the house and trees were cut to pieces by cannon and minnie-balls." Beaverdam was occupied by Ripley's Brigade of D. H. Hill's Division and by Pender's Brigade of A. P. Hill's.

The home was been remodeled and is now occupied by Mrs. Roy Rogers, Sr. The surrounding area is now known as Beaverdam Park and is a subdivision.

Buckeye, *Pamunkey Woman's Club Calendar,* July 1989, by Sandi McVeigh
Calhoun.

Buckeye

Built in the early eighteenth century, some authorities suggesting 1720,
Buckeye stands as one of the oldest standing historic landmarks of Hanover
County. The house is typical of the early building in Tidewater Virginia
and consists of one-and-a-half stories of wood placed on a brick basement.
It is noted for its modillion cornice and its interior woodwork.

It is believed that Buckeye was built by William Pollard, second clerk
of the Hanover County Court from 1740 to his death in 1781. Pollard was
the son of Joseph Pollard (1701-1791) of King and Queen County, later of
Goochland, who married Priscilla Hoomes, of The Old Mansion, Caroline
County. Joseph Pollard (1701-1791) was the son of Robert Pollard of
Bruington, King and Queen County. According to tradition, the first clerk's
office of Hanover County stood in the yard of Buckeye.

William Pollard was active in the Hanover County of his day and
married Mary Anderson by whom he had five sons and five daughters.
One of his sons, William Pollard, junior, became clerk of the court after
his father's death and served until 1829. He lived at Williamsville in
Hanover County. Another son, Thomas, lived at Courtland, near Hanover
Court House and served as clerk of the Circuit Court from 1819 to 1829.

Apparently, Buckeye passed into the possession of Benjamin Pollard, another son of William Pollard.

Benjamin Pollard, known as "Ben Trusty," lived and died at Buckeye. He served at one time as clerk of Accomac County and owned two lots in the town of Accomac from 1790-1793. He probably moved back to Hanover after 1793 and later served as clerk of the Circuit Court of the City of Richmond. Benjamin Pollard and was the father of William Thomas Henry Pollard. Buckeye next passed into the hands of William T. H. Pollard (died circa 1856), clerk of the Circuit Court of Hanover County from 1851 until his death. William T. H. Pollard married on Tuesday evening, 20 December 1831, in the Episcopal Church in Hanover, Miss Susan Catherine Winston.

W. T. H. Pollard died at Buckeye circa 1856, leaving a will (4 January 1853, recorded 22 July 1856) by which he wished, after the payment of his debts his estate to be "kept together for the support of my wife and children..." He further made the benevolent request that "none of his negroes under the age of 14 years...be hired out unless it be such as go with their Mothers and none of them put on public works except with the approbation of my wife."

Mrs. Pollard continued to live at Buckeye until her death there 7 Jul 1881 at the age of seventy. On 10 Mar 1864 she saw her daughter, Williana Overton Pollard (1844-1890) marry Doctor Thomas E. Williams of Clarke County. Mrs. Pollard may have spent some of her last years in Richmond for on 22 December 1865 some of their personal property in the estate of her husband along with certain pieces of farm equipment and live stock was auctioned off. At the time it was mentioned that the items sold contained "all the property not removed by Mrs. Susan C. Pollard, which was considered necessary for her comfort in Richmond."

After the death of Mrs. W. T. H. Pollard in 1881 the Buckeye property descended to her heirs. To settle the estate, George P. Haw was appointed special commissioner and sold 438½ acres "known and called Buck Eye" to Carter Scott Anderson on 6 April 1883. Carter Scott Anderson (died 1918 in Richmond) had married Alice B. Pollard (1847-1926), daughter of William T. H. and Susan C. Pollard on 18 May 1868 in Halifax, North Carolina. In 1905 Captain Carter Scott Anderson sold part of the Buckeye tract reserving a plot of eighty acres around the house. At his death in 1918 he left the property to his two daughters, Mary Carter Anderson and Katherine Winston Anderson. At their mother's death in 1926 the "farm Buckeye was left to Mary Carter Anderson, the wife of Charles S. Gardner."

Mrs. Gardner with her brother and sister sold the Buckeye property to Mrs. Charles Simpson in 1928. However, the property came back on the market in 1930 and Mary Anderson Gardner re-purchased the old home place. Mrs. Gardner held Buckeye for a year and sold the place with approximately eighty acres in 1931 to William W. Crowe. This ended an approximately two hundred year old association of the Pollard family with Buckeye.

In 1942 William W. Crowe and his wife sold the property to Eleanor Folsom Dyer who, in turn, sold the place to Henry S. Winston, Jr., in 1954. Mr. Winston sold Buckeye to the present owners, Doctor and Mrs. Charles W. Massey in 1962. The Masseys have continued the preservation work started by earlier owners and retained the gracious charm of this historic landmark of Hanover County.

J. R. Fishburn, Virginia Historic Landmarks Commission

This article was substitued for the article in *Old Homes of Hanover County Virginia and was taken from Hanover County Historical Society Bulletin,* No. 1, November 1969

Courtland. Drawing by Edith Schermerhorn. Courtesy of the Hanover County Historical Society.

Courtland

Named for its proximity to Hanover Courthouse, this was an early home of the Pollard family sold to William Overton Winston about 1842. William Overton and his wife Sarah had boarded with the Pollards when they first married. He was a deputy County Clerk under his father who had served almost a lifetime.

This is a working farm which includes the main house and the usual outbuildings, including an old spring house which covers the spring that supplies water to the whole farm. There is a brick-walled cemetery from the Pollard's time that had three stones: Rebecca Bacon Pollard 1780-1844; Thomas Pollard1768-1830; and Mary A. J., consort of Henry A. Temple and daughter of Thomas and Rebecca Pollard 1806-1831.

The Winston's son, Philip Bickerton, at 17 enlisted in Co. E., Fifth Virginia Cavalry and served as a courier to Colonel Thomas Rosser, who was later to become his brother-in-law. Philip became Captain on Rosser's staff when the Colonel became Brigadier General. General Custer of "Custer's Last Stand" fame was a West Point friend of General Rosser. Several times during the war Courtland had been headquarters for General Custer but he reportedly sent a guard ahead to protect the home.

During the battle of Hanover Courthouse the Federal Troops were on the courthouse hill and the Confederates placed their guns in Courtland yard. They were asked to move them so the house would not be damaged. After the surrender of both Lee and Johnston, General John Logan camped at Courtland. Mrs. Winston, who was a widow with seven children, had spent what little gold she had managed to save in buying mules with which to work the farm. When Logan left he took every live animal on the place including the bird dog.

After the war Philip Bickerton Winston returned to Courtland to farm and support his mother, brothers, and sisters. His brother, Fendall, went west with General Rosser and became successful and wealthy.

Betty Barbara Winston Rosser bought the place from her mother and owned it for two years, selling it to Philip Bickerton. The night after the deed was signed the house burned. The family, seeing the house could not be saved, ordered the dinner table, with all the food on it, moved to the lawn where it is said they finished their dinner. The house was quickly rebuilt.

When Philip Bickerton Winston was away, Bickerton Lyle Winston, his brother, who was the doctor in the community, farmed the place for him. In 1872 Philip Bickerton left Virginia, becoming a successful businessman and a respected politician in Minnesota. He kept Courtland until 1927, when it was sold to Dr. Boatwright, later president of the University of Richmond. The house burned again, and in 1937 was again rebuilt by a new owner, John W. Whaley, who used the unburnt story-and-a-half schoolhouse as a wing and added a two-story house, making use of the bricks from the houses that had burned in the past.

Courtland was purchased in 1966 by Dr. Richard Kennon Williams from the estate of the late Mr. Whaley. The Williams have carried on Courtland's gracious hospitality and beauty.

Dundee. *Pamunkey Woman's Club Calendar*, May 2007, by Pat Jeffress.

Dundee

Dundee was first owned by Samuel Gist who came into possession of the property when he married the widow of John Smith (died 1746), a large land owner who lived at Gould Hill. The original Dundee house which was standing in 1768 is no longer. The late Miss Mary Haw who lived at Dundee stated that the brick foundations of the old Dundee are on the hill behind the present house. In 1768, Dundee was mentioned in a letter from Samuel Gist in London to his step-son, John Smith, Jr., suggesting he rent Dundee House, if possible. Samuel Gist and his wife Mary, had one daughter, Mary Gist, who married first William Anderson of Hanover. By 1778, William Anderson, Gent., was of Dundee.

The present Dundee home was built about 1810-1820 by Thomas Price, Jr. of Cool Water. The wings were added in 1840. One wing was used as a school room for the English tutor, Miss Louisa Webb. See *Hanover County Historical Society Bulletin* No. 9, November 1973 for letter written by Miss Webb in 1861 when she was living with the William O. Winston family.

Thomas Price Jr. had a son, Dr. Lucien Price whose daughter married George Haw, Sr. of Haw's Shop (Studley) and Dundee next came into possession of the Haw family in whose possession it remains today.

The home is of old English bond. The front entrance is through heavy double five-panel doors with fan transom and side lights. The English basement is only two-feet deep below ground level, with heart pine floors. There are twelve rooms with beautiful mantels carved and fluted with small alcoves on each side on the first floor. There is a secret stairway leading from the east room on the second floor to the attic. The inside doors are heavy six panel cross type, heart pine and poplar. It was a camping ground for both armies in the Civil War and Dundee shows marks by bullets from both sides. General J. E. B. Stuart and Major Heros von Borcke were frequent visitors here. This lovely old home is located on Route 605 not far from the Courthouse, off Rte. 301.

Garthright House. *Pamunkey Regional Woman's Club Calender,* December 2017, by John Augustus Walters.

Garthright House

There is no authentic information as to the early construction of this old home. It was built in two sections, one of brick and one of frame. It was used for a hospital during one of the bloodiest battles of the Civil War, as it was located at, or very near, the Cold Harbor battlefield. The National Cemetery is located across the road. These two landmarks are on the battlefield tour of the Civil War around Richmond. In May 1970, the house was heavily damaged by fire which originated at the ground level in the back of the house and burned upward in a two-foot wide area until it reached the second floor and roof. However, it was not damaged beyond repair and the National Park Service has restored the house to its original appearance.

The first known occupants of this old home were Miles Garthright and his wife, Margaret E., who were living here at the time of the Civil War. He was deceased by 1896 when deeds were given for several tracts of land "at Cold Harbor National Cemetery" to settle his estate. One tract was for 55 acres, and the other was for 120 acres, joining the lands of Joseph T. Martin, south by the lands of Patsy Bowe and McGhee, west by William H. Grubbs. The second named tract (120 acres) included an enclosed graveyard and a "strip of 20-ft. on every side of the enclosure is reserved as a family burying ground for the use of all parties to this deed and their families." The bricked graveyard can still be seen today, but there are no tombstones.

This tract was deeded to Margaret E. Yarbrough and Alice F. Ratcliffe, daughters of Miles Garthright, who were to take and hold as co-partners for their portion of Miles Garthright's estate, thus becoming the next owners of this old home. Walter C. Garthright, Miles' son, received the land located on the north side of the county road (the 55 acres) joining the National Cemetery. Miles and Margaret Garthright had three children: Walter C. of Richmond; Margaret E, wife of George Yarbrough; and Alice F., wife of Hampden F. Ratcliff. The daughter of George and Margaret (Garthright) Yarbrough. conveyed to Maggie E. McGhee in 1925 – "and hereby agree that the old dwelling house, now situated on the property known as the Garthright Home, and which was used as a hospital during the Civil War, will not be moved off the property, but will remain on the present site as evidenced by their accepting and recording this deed."

And thus we have this old historic home, preserved by the Richmond Battlefield Parks to visit, and which is another "monument" to all the wounded and dying men who took part in this bloody campaign of Cold Harbor.

[Note: This was originally a Hooper family home as noted in the Hooper articles. The half-rounded brick-walled cemetery contains James Hooper.]

Kidd Home. May 2, 1886. Dr. Francis Lord Collection at U. S. Army Military History Institute.

"Spring Hill"
Kidd Home/Adams House

The original caption for above picture when taken in 1886: "The Adams House near Gaines' Mill, Va., May 2, 1886 on the battlefield of June 27, 1862. The old lady on the stoop is Mrs. Adams who was present in the cellar of the house on the day of the battle of Gains [sic] Mill, June 27, 1862."

From just before the Civil War to present, the land on which this house stood has been owned by the Adams family. According to the late Edwin Adams, the house had fallen down by 1950, and today, the ruins including both collapsed chimneys and filled-in basement have been covered over.

Pitman Kidd (ca 1755, Essex County, VA – ca 1807, Hanover County, VA) married Mary Austin (23 Jan 1763, Hanover County, VA – ca 1797, Hanover County, VA) married ca Feb 1784, Hanover County, VA. The marriage is based on the birth date of eldest daughter Sarah Bohannon Kidd (15 Dec 1784, Hanover County, VA – 22 Apr 1862, Hanover County, VA). Mary Crenshaw Kidd (1785 – 1834) was their only other known child. Pitman (1725 – 1770) was the son of and Sarah Bohannon (1775 – 1782), all of Essex County, VA. Mary Austin was the daughter of John Austin, Sr. (1726 – 1815) and Mary Crenshaw (1726 – 1763), all of Hanover County.

Pitman Kidd's mother died ca 1782, and shortly thereafter in 1783, he began selling his land in Essex County. That same year, he appears in the

Hanover County land and personal property tax records. Based on this sequence of events, including his estimated marriage date, it is believed the Pitman Kidd house as pictured, was built ca 1783.

Pitman Kidd's will dated 3 Nov 1806, naming his second wife Agnes [Richardson] Sharp (1767 – ca 1845), his two daughters and others, was offered at probate 25 May 1808, in Hanover County by one of his executors and son-in-law, John Jones (ca 1783, England – 22 Oct 1833, Hanover County, VA), Mary C. Kidd's husband. His estate was settled 26 Jan 1831, with each daughter receiving 360 acres of land, Sarah Bohannon Kidd and Hugh Watt receiving "lot No. 2" with their house Springfield/Watt House by the luck of the draw, Sarah having drawn first. John and Mary Jones, having substantial wealth, sold their 360 acres "lot No. 1" "exclusive of one quarter of an acre, square around the burying ground, rather the grave yard of said dec'd [Pitman Kidd] to be herein after laid out." In 1835, William Austin Jones (1815 – 1840), son of John and Mary C. Jones, purchased it and probably lived there. After his death, Joseph Adams became the eventual owner of the then called "Spring Hill" 360 acre tract with the Pitman Kidd house and outbuildings.

The house based on field work of the ruins by Ashley Neville and Art Taylor on 26 Jan 2002, was 36 feet x 16 feet, with English basement, two room first floor and half story second floor. The stairs were located inside the off centered front door to the west. The two standing chimneys showed evidence of repair/rebuild over the years with fireplaces in each chimney for both floors. The west chimney had an additional fireplace in basement. Basement walls were 14 – 16 inches thick, laid primarily English bond.

The cemetery was the "Kidd" cemetery and no Adams were buried in it. The Adams family cemetery is located in then a hedge row almost immediately behind of the Kidd home site and the slave cemetery was located in the same hedgerow just east of the Adams cemetery. Typical grave depressions were visible. These cemeteries are accessible only with owner permission.

Readers may be interested in the "Watt Family Bible" records are in the book, and the "Bible Records of Hugh and Margaret [Mills] Watt of Glenarm, County Antrim, Ireland" which includes Kidd – Watt Cemetery.

Article Note

1. *Hanover County Historical Society Bulletin*, Vol. 1, pp. 165-167 & *Hanover County Historical Society Bulletin*, Vol. II, pp.6, 26,124-125, 201-204 and 206.

2. Hanover Historical Society. *Old Homes Book of Hanover County, Virginia*, Salem, VA: Walsworth Publishing Company, 1983, pages 124 – 125.

Laurel Meadow. *Pamunkey Woman's Club Calendar,* September 1989, by M. A. Pennington.

Laurel Meadow

In Patent Book 8, page 245, a land patent to Rice Hughes 29 April 1693 mentioned the land of George Polegreen on Beaverdam Swamp, which is believed to be the same land on which the home, Laurel Meadow, was later built. This old home is an English type farmhouse dating back to the Colonial era. The exact date is unknown. It has no center hall but stands a story-and-a-half above a full English basement in which the dining room and kitchen are located. The house has hand-hewn beams and the original wide floor boards, all of heart pine.

A plat plan shows Laurel Meadow in 1821 adjoining White Chimneys plantation both of which were owned by Isaac Oliver. Of the 1,139 acres shown on the plat, including a grist mill, 879 are depicted thereon as being in the Laurel Meadow tract and 260 is the White Chimneys tract. There were Olivers in Hanover County early; Isaac Oliver was a son of Benjamin Oliver, a descendant of one of these early; Olivers. Tax records show he had his own housekeeping establishment in 1809. From the estate of Benjamin Oliver, Sr. who died in 1819 or 1820, Isaac Oliver received 879 acres which included the Laurel Meadow tract adjacent to White Chimneys, which he already owned. Isaac Oliver died ca. 1831 and Ann A. Oliver, his wife, retained Laurel Meadow until 1848 when it passed into the hands of Elizabeth H. Miller who sold it to George K. Hundley in 1860.

During the Civil War the home was occupied by both Federal and Confederate troops. A descendant of the first Hundley to own Laurel

Meadow and who lived here during that period, reported that General Stonewall Jackson spent the night there in 1862 and met General Lee at Walnut Grove Church the following morning; and that General Jackson did not sleep in the room assigned to him but spent the night in the dining room writing *Dispatch*es. Trenches and artillery emplacements are still in place from the Polegreen skirmish on June 1, 1864.

After holding the property about 40 years, the Hundleys sold it to John W. and Catherine L. Simpkins who five years later conveyed it to Ella H. Shelton. The next owner was James A. McGhee; and in 1937 it was sold to the present owners, James B. and Mary N. Spratley. Laurel Meadow is located off Meadowbridge Road (Route 627), also known as Polegreen Road.

Locust Hill. Thought to be drawn by Robert Alonzo Brock and published here for the first time.

Locust Hill

The pencil sketch of Locust Hill (sometimes referred to as Locust Grove or Locust Level) is attributed to Robert Alonzo Brock, a noted newspaper editor, writer, and genealogist who married Sallie Kidd Haw, daughter of Richardson Tyree Haw and Margaret Mills Watt, daughter of Hugh Watt and Sarah Bohannon Kidd. A note accompanying the sketch indicates that the Locust Hill tract was once part of Studley. The dwelling had fallen down by 1932.

Research by Art Taylor and Allan Smith indicates that the house was probably located on the east side of Summer Hill Road, north of Salem Church. This is documented in a Haw vs. Haw suit in Hanover County Chancery Records in an Indenture dated 13 Apr 1838 between Richardson T. Haw and John Haw, both of Hanover County, as "on the road leading from Salem Church to Hanover Town, bounded on the north by said road, on the east by the lands of Miss Anderson, Reuben Gardner, and Judge Brokenbrough [sic], on the south by the land of Doctor Talley, and on the west by the land of Reuben Gardner, and is the same tract or parcel of land on which the said Richardson T. Haw presently resides on, containing three hundred and fifteen acres be the same however more or less." Further in the suit, it is noted that this 314¼ acres was deeded to Richardson T. Haw by Peter Lyons, 17 Apr 1832. John Haw deeded 50 acres to E. S. Talley sometime between his acquiring the land and the suit, thus the 265¼ acres advertised for Commissioner's Sale on 19 Jun 1878. The handbill printed by the *Richmond Whig* described Locust Hill as "situated in a healthy neighborhood, convenient to Churches, Schools, Stores, Shops, and Mills; is about 15 miles from Richmond, and within 8 miles of the C&O Railroad. It has on it a good dwelling house with six rooms and other buildings necessary and useful to farm. About one-half of this land is cleared, and in good farm and truck land, and about half is in fine wood and timber of first quality." The ultimate sale of Locust Hill was to Richardson Wallace Haw, son of Richardson Tyree. Haw, with proceeds distributed among the children of Richardson T. Haw.

Marlbourne. *Pamunkey Woman's Club Calendar;* June 1987, by Virginia Randolph
Parrish.

Marlbourne

Marlbourne, located about one mile from Old Church in lower Hanover
County, was long the home of Edmund Ruffin, noted States-Righter and
agriculturist. The house was built 1839-40 by Bartholomew McC. Tomlin on
property formerly belonging to his wife's family, the Blakeys. Mr. Tomlin
sold the farm in 1843 to Edmund Ruffin who promptly named the place
Marlbourne in deference to his success in experiments with marl. Edmund
Ruffin, his wife, Susan Travis Ruffin, and children moved to Marlbourne on
New Year's Day in 1844 from his Coggins Point property in Prince George
County. Within a few years Ruffin had transformed the run-down, poorly
drained property into an agricultural showplace, again emphasizing his
theories on proper farming methods and marling and their success.

The Marlbourne house is built along traditional Virginia lines, two
stories, one room deep, with a center hall and end chimney, and wings
extended on each side. The parlor on the left with library beyond, the
dining room on the right and chamber all contain handsome woodwork,
mantles and wainscoting. Graceful triple windows light the parlor and
dining rooms. A two-story porch faces the carriage drive with a similar
porch on the rear, or north side, overlooking the farm land extending to the

Pamunkey River. This view, one of the most extensive in eastern Virginia, is in Ruffin's words, "a prospect of rare beauty."

In 1856 Edmund Ruffin retired from farming and divided among his children all his landed property, but reserved Marlbourne for his lifetime. Two of the sons, Edmund, Jr., and Julian C. Ruffin, purchased the shares of the other children in the Marlbourne property. Lower Hanover County saw much heavy fighting during the Civil War, and as the home of a Southern spokesman, Marlbourne suffered heavily. Family letters describe the desolation found there after the family refuged to Amelia County. Following the news of Lee's surrender at Appomattox, Ruffin took his own life and lies buried in the Ruffin family grave yard on a hill overlooking his beloved farmland. In a property division following the war, Julian's widow, Charlotte Meade Ruffin, inherited the lower portion of the farm, including the house, and lived here for more than fifty years until her death in 1918. Her son, Julian Meade Ruffin, only 12 at the time the war ended, began farming for his widowed mother several years following the Civil War at the age of 16, and continued for many years to manage the property. At Charlotte Meade Ruffin's death, Marlbourne became the home of her daughter, Bessie Ruffin Broaddus. Mrs. Broaddus' son, A. Woodford Broaddus inherited Marlbourne at his mother's death. The place is now owned by his widow, Jane Campbell Broaddus's, and her son, Tilghman.

Marlbourne is on the Virginia Landmarks Register and is a Registered National Historic Landmark. It is also the recipient of the Bronze Plaque.

Meadow Farm. *Pamunkey Woman's Club Calendar*, October 1991, by Virginia Singleton Darnell.

Meadow Farm

This old home is located off Cold Harbor Road, not far from the Chickahominy River and Beaverdam Creek, near the historical area of Cold Harbor. The original house was a two-story log cabin, two rooms up and two rooms down. It has been enlarged from time to time; the original four rooms becoming a part of the larger house. During this century when the house was again being remodeled, the original logs were uncovered. Today the house consists of sixteen rooms with a half-basement and full attic. There was an old wine cellar and a sub-basement used as a root cellar. The foundation bricks and chimney were made on the place. The house has been pegged together and the wooden dowels can be seen in the staircase and other areas. Blood stains can still be seen on the original flooring where the wounded were cared for during the Battle of Cold Harbor.

Meadow Farm was the home of the family of William B. Sydnor (1806-1862) and his wife, Sarah T. Austin (1812-1879). He was the son of Edward Garland Sydnor (b. 1769) and his wife, Sally White (b. ca. 1775). Sarah (Austin) Sydnor was the daughter of William Smith Austin (1788-1866) and his wife, Nancy Winn (1794-1849). These families were neighbors, the Austin's living at Walnut Lane which adjoined Meadow Farm on Cold

Harbor Road and also adjoined Oakley Hill where William B. Sydnor's brother, Edward, lived.

William B. Sydnor ran a school here before the Civil War. The site is near the entrance to the house, marked by trees. In the *Richmond Whig* (semi-weekly) January 6, 1846, this ad appeared:

Meadow Farm Seminary. The exercises of this school will be resumed under the superintendence of Mr. W.B. Langridge on the 12th inst. and close 12th December following with a vacation of one month in the summer. Terms -- For board $80; for tuition in Latin, Greek, and Mathematics $30; in English from $15 to $25 according to the advancement of the pupil.

--W. B. Sydnor

Meadow Farm and the Sydnor family played an important role in the organization of Walnut Grove Baptist Church. Mr. Edward Sydnor, of Oakley Hill, gave the land in 1845 on which the church now stands. The school was also the site where the Baptist congregation sometimes met before the church was built.

An interesting article in *The Religious Herald* of 1921, written by Henry Clinton Sydnor, the young son of William B. and Sarah T. Sydnor, tells of the family experiences during the Civil War when the Battles of Cold Harbor, Ellerson's Mill and Mechanicsville were being fought all around Meadow Farm which was only one mile from Ellerson's Mill. William B. Sydnor sent away many members of his family; only a daughter, a son, his wife, and himself remained. This family had sixteen children, five of whom were in the Confederate Army. "The Federal officers and soldiers erected tents everywhere and telegraph wires were tacked to the trees. The wagons, each drawn by four fine mules seemed to be in the thousands. The barn was also taken over as headquarters for the men who did picket duty on the Chickahominy River." The family was confined to the immediate surroundings and the officers told Mr. Sydnor they would respect his family and not willfully destroy his property. After the Yankees left, Longstreet's men passed through on their way to Cold Harbor, two miles distance. According to tradition, Robert E. Lee also visited Meadow Farm on his way to rendezvous with "Stonewall" Jackson at Walnut Grove Church. In 1908 it came into the possession of Jessie L. Dodsworth.

This home will also be remembered for the camp operated by Mr. and Mrs. Caleb Dodsworth for boys and girls for many years with youths attending from all over the country, most of whom were impressed with the historical aspects of the home, as well as the surrounding area, where many men fell during the fierce fighting which took place in the area.

Oak Grove. *Pamunkey Woman's Club calendar*, August 1991, by Nancy Liesfeld Cozart.

Oak Grove and Locust Grove [Locust Hill]

Oak Grove is one of two homes of John Haw. It was the home of his grandson, Richardson Tyree Haw (1809-1849) who married 1831, Margaret Mills Watt (1811-1878), daughter of Hugh Watt and Sarah B. (Kidd) Watt of the Watt House. Locust Grove burned many years ago and the exact location in the Studley area is unknown, other than it was within a mile of Oak Grove. [See Locust Hill.] Richardson T. and Margaret Watt had seven daughters and two sons; one son, Richardson W. Haw, served in the Civil War along with his five double first cousins.

Oak Grove was the home of another grandson, John Haw, III, brother of Richardson T. Haw. He married Mary Austin Watt, sister to Margaret Mills Watt. They had two daughters and five sons, all five sons served in the Civil War. It is believed that this house was built about 1785-1790 by John Haw III and from whose family Haw's Shop or Hawsville was named. Later, this area was changed to Studley in honor of the historic plantation where Patrick Henry was born, and which property adjoined Oak Grove. It was John Haw who invented the circular saw here and which was manufactured at Haw's Shop, along with other farming equipment. The shop was located opposite the Studley Post Office. When the Civil War began, he sold his equipment to the Tredegar Iron Works in Richmond.

John and Mary (Watt) Haw had five sons in the Confederate Army: John H. Haw, Sgt. William Haw, Edwin Haw, Joseph R. Haw and George P. Haw. One son, George Pitman Haw (b. 1838) lost his left arm at

Sharpsburg. After the Civil War he entered Washington College (now Washington and Lee University) and was Commonwealth Attorney for Hanover County for more than thirty years. After his retirement he lived at Dundee with his daughter. The Haw family gave the land on which both Enon Methodist Church and Salem Presbyterian Church. are built. Oak Grove is the typical early Virginia home, with English basement, two rooms on the upper floors, one on each side of a center hall, one-room deep. The present owners, Mr. and Mrs. John Spiers, have added on and remodeled the rear of the home. Original mantels and floors have been well preserved. This home remained in the Haw family until 1940. Miss Nannie Haw being the last member of the Haw family to live here, when it was sold to Mr. and Mr. L. Otis Spiers who in turn passed the property to their son, John.

Oak Grove was near the severe fighting which took place at Enon Church on May 28, 1864 and was used as a hospital. In the yard can be seen a tombstone of a Texas soldier erected by the soldier's family.

Pointer's or David Woody's. *Pamunkey Woman's Club Calendar,* June 1996, by Carol A. Bock.

Pointer's or David Woody's

This well preserved home located near old Cold Harbor was once the property of David Woody (b. 1802) and which was valued on the 1850 census at $2,000, indicating the house was standing at that time. David Woody owned several adjoining tracts, one of which came into the possession of the William Warren family, whose son, John H. Warren (b. 1842) and his wife, Mary E., sold to Charles D. Woody (son of David). By 1899, Charles David Woody sold to Margaret E. Boze (Mrs. Henry Boze) of Richmond, who, in turn, deeded the property in 1931 to William Henry Boze, her son, citing 103 acres, 50 conveyed to Charles David Woody by John H. Warren and 53 acres by Charles David Woody from his father. The property has changed hands since that date, and since 1970 it has been the home of Mr. and Mrs. W. H. Pointer, Jr.

It was David Woody who gave the land on which Beulah Presbyterian Church stands. The church is believed to have been built in the 1840's. It burned during the Civil War and was rebuilt about 1869. David Woody was a leader in the community during his lifetime. His home must have been in the line of fire during the battle of Cold Harbor, as it is located on Route 633 [Beulah Church Road] near old Cold Harbor, next to Beulah Presbyterian Church.

Powhite. Historic American Building Survey, 1933.

Powhite

This old home, no longer standing, was, in its day, quite a showplace, and occupied by prominent families in Hanover. Powhite was at one time a part of the William Macon tract (see Fairfield) of 2,658 acres in 1782. In 1801 Thomas Macon conveyed to James Govan, of King and Queen County, 871 acres which was known as Powhite. James Govan (1754-1831) was the immigrant ancestor of the Govans of King William, King & Queen and Hanover Counties. He married Elizabeth Gaines, daughter of Francis Gaines of King and Queen. James purchased Powhite about 1822 and died there in 1831. Two of his sons, Edward and Archibald, settled in Hanover, Edward at Powhite and Archibald at Selwyn, the adjoining farm and which may have been a part of Powhite at that time. By 1834, Edward Govan had 1,146 acres and was indebted to his brothers, James Govan, Jr. and Archibald, for $9,000 "...said bonds made in consideration of the purchase of Powhite tract by said Edward Govan ... same tract conveyed by Executor of James Govan (Sr.) and at which land the said Edward Govan resides..." This was a Deed of Trust to Henry Curtis and William Trueheart. Later, Powhite was advertised for sale and described in a newspaper advertisement as a large and commodious dwelling house, extensive barns and all other outhouses, a spacious garden with orchards and select fruit, and 666 acres. William F. Gaines must have purchased the estate at this time as he was in possession of it by 1845.

The Govan family may have had a school at Powhite prior to 1845, as the *Richmond Whig and Public Advertiser* of January 6, 1846 ran an ad which stated: "This school will be re-opened on the 15th January and close on 14th December (1846). A few boarders will be taken and they must furnish their own towels ... utmost attention will be paid to the moral deportment and comfort of the young ladies entrusted to our care." Also included in the ad, "Board and tuition in English $110; French $10; Music and use of instrument $35;" and signed by Wm. F. Gaines.

From this time on until the Civil War, Powhite was owned by the Gaines family, and from whom the famous mill received its name. William F. Gaines died May 1874 and after his ownership Powhite was occupied by many families. The Edward Graves family is the present owner and has been since the 1940's. The original home has been destroyed but the bricks from the four massive chimneys were used in the construction of the house of Mrs. Graves.

The old house was 50' wide and 28' deep with front and back porches across the entire house, 8' wide. The floors were eight and ten inch heart pine and poplar. It was two-rooms deep on each side of a central stairway, averaging about 14 x 20 feet. In the rear was a terraced garden of fine old boxwoods. Slightly northeast of the house was an old brick munitions house 30' wide x 50' long with gabled roof.

Powhite was the home of Frances Gaines (Mrs. Seaton Garland Tinsley) who was the author of the Civil War diary in which she tells of the hardships the neighbors endured during the Civil War. The Union soldiers occupied the yard and surrounding countryside, and the Gaines family were prisoners in their own home.

Puccoon. Courtesy of Library of Virginia.

Puccoon

Puccoon was located on Cold Harbor Road across from Fairfield, the old Macon home. It was known for many years as the home of Dr. Henry Curtis who was a distinguished and respected citizen of this area of Hanover for many years. Dr. Curtis was born in Boston, Massachusetts, March 18, 1792, and moved to Virginia, near Petersburg, with his widowed mother, when a young lad. He was a student of medicine at the University of Maryland where he graduated May 4, 1812, and moved to Hanover County by July 1, 1812, according to his business card. This was soon after the death of his friend, Dr. Thomas Chrystie, who had died in February 1812. He lived in, or near, Hanover Town until he purchased Puccoon from William Macon of Fairfield December 30, 1820, consisting then of 537-1/2 acres, and he may have been the builder of this home. The name Puccoon came from a weed that grew profusely on the place and from which the Indians made paint. He married Christiana Booth Tyler, daughter of Governor (and Judge) John Tyler June 27, 1813. The house had six panel doors of two-inch heart pine, and had the original wrought iron hinges and locks. The downstairs rooms had wainscoting three-feet high and one-and-one-half inches thick of pine and poplar. It had wide beaded weather boarding of heavy heart pine. The house was built in two phases. The portion with the front stoop and dormers is the oldest section.

Puccoon was in the line of fire during the Battle of Gaines' Mill and Cold Harbor. There were scars on the window ledge and door jamb caused by a cannon ball that came in the room where Dr. Curtis lay in bed ill, but it did not explode.

The will of Dr. Curtis was dated June 1, 1855, in which he mentioned his children and some grandchildren. He mentioned his service in the War of 1812, leaving his bounty land warrant for this service to his son, Tyler Curtis. Dr. Curtis died July 31, 1862. Both he and his wife were buried at Puccoon, but later they were re-interred in Forest Lawn Cemetery in Richmond. In 1865, the homestead tract was owned and occupied by Dr. B. A. Curtis and Maria A. Curtis, his wife. The home was owned by the G. A. Foster family when it burned in the 1950.

Rural Plains. *Pamunkey Woman's Club Calendar,* September 1986, by J. Berle McGhee.

Rural Plains

This home is one of the oldest -- if not the oldest -- in Hanover County. It not only has connections to Hanover's historic past, but also to the Commonwealth of Virginia. It has been the home of seven proven generations of Shelton's and probably that of nine. The home is better known as the site of the wedding of Patrick Henry and Sarah Shelton in 1754. According to the Historic Landmarks Commission, Rural Plains ... is a handsome specimen of a substantial, non-academic rural Virginia farmhouse. It is noteworthy both for its mid-eighteenth century brickwork and for its long tenure in the Shelton family.

At the entrance to Rural Plains is a marker erected by the Hanover Branch of the APVA in 1932, which gives a bit of additional history connected to this area: In 1656 Totopotomoi, Chief of the Pamunkey Indians, a faithful ally of the English, was killed in the Battle of Bloody Run near Richmond. Rural Plains borders Totopotomoy Creek. In 1754 Rural Plains was the scene of the marriage of Patrick Henry and Sarah Shelton; and in 1864 the Battle of Totopotomoy took place preceding Cold Harbor.

The fireplace before which Sarah Shelton and Patrick Henry were married is on an angle between two walls so that the huge chimney might accommodate flues from other parts of the house. The mantel, like most of the woodwork, is original heart of pine. The floors on the second floor are original. Basement walls are three feet thick; above they are one-and-a-half feet thick. The brick walls above the basement level are eighteen inches thick. The original cypress shingled Dutch mansard roof was riddled under bombardment during the Civil War and has been replaced. Signs of cannon damage can still be seen on the back wall of the house. Also, initials have been carved in the old bricks, initials of the Civil War soldiers camped on the property.

There are two chimneys, one at each end, five-feet at the base and three feel thick. The house has thirteen rooms, four on each floor with a ten-foot center hall.

General John Hancock of the Union Army made his headquarters here. He had suggested to the Shelton family to leave the area, but Mrs. Shelton refused due to illness of a daughter and they were forced to stay in the basement. Col. Edwin Shelton (1798-1874) who was born here, married in 1827 Sarah Elizabeth Oliver (1810-1887), and it was their family who lived here during the Civil War, and who were confined to the basement during the fighting at Haw's Shop and the Battle of Totopotomoy Creek.

Col. Edwin Shelton was the son of Capt. John Shelton, a Revolutionary War solider, who married Ann Southall in 1784. The present owner is William R. Shelton, Jr., the seventh proven generation of Sheltons to live in, and take care of, this old home located on Route 606, Studley Road. Rural Plains is listed on both the Virginia Landmarks Register and the National Register of Historic Places. It is also on the Virginia Farm Bureau Bicentennial Farm Register of farms which have been in the same family for two hundred years.

[The house is now owned by the National Park Service at the bequest of Mr. Shelton.]

Signal Hill or Lindley. *Pamunkey Woman's Club Calendar,* November, 1986, by James H. Rodgers.

Signal Hill or Lindley

Lindley, called Signal Hill after the Civil War because of its signal station during that conflict, is a well preserved old home which belonged to the Winston family. It was probably built around 1840, or earlier. It is located on Route 301 adjoining the cemetery of the same name. The Bickerton Lyle Winston family lived here during the Civil War, having moved back to Hanover County from Richmond after 1850. His family is shown on the 1850 census of Richmond and Henrico County. He and John R. Winston of Richmond had twenty-two acres in the 1840's and by 1863 Bickerton L. Winston is shown with 354-1/2 acres adjoining L. B. Price (Dundee) and 237-1/2 acres adjoining H. Cady.

Bickerton L. Winston (1816-1902) was the son of Philip Bickerton Winston (1786-1853) and his first wife, Sarah Madison Pendleton; and brother of William O. Winston of Courtland. He married (1) 1846 Catherine Louise Newton who died 1856 and by whom he had two daughters, Jane P. and Margaret Winston. He married (2) Elizabeth (Betty) Minor Bankhead who survived him and who was willed Signal Hill in 1902.

Signal Hill is frame over an English basement. There are two rooms 18 x 20 feet on each side of a center hall on both the first and second floors. The hall is 12 feet wide and 36 feet long. The windows are long, coming down to floor level. There are porches on the back, both up and down, the length of the house. During the Civil War the home was used as a signal station at the battle of Hanover Courthouse, hence the name. The Union troops slept in the hall while the Winston family were being held "prisoners" in their home.

In the yard is a frame two-story house referred to as the surveyor's home, and where the slaves reported. The stairway has hand-hewed boards along the right-hand walls. There are two rooms up and two down. This home was built about 1860.

After the Winston's occupancy, it was purchased at auction in 1922 by Boxley Vaughan and from him to G. F. Vaughan in 1939, who in turn deeded the property to Robert J. Lindquist. The next owner was Mrs. T. Hunter Dougherty who left it to Carson-Newman College. The present owners are Mr. and Mrs. Gordon Lawhorn.

Totomoi. *Pamunkey Woman's Club Calendar, July,* 1991, by William Calvert Perrine.

Totomoi

Note: This article was written by Maria W. Rippe and used with her permission.

According to Nugent's abstracts of Virginia's colonial patent records, the land known in 2009 as Totomoi Farm was once included in a 1,206-acre patent issued to George Wilkinson and John Wilkinson in 1703. At that time, the patent was located in St. Peter's Parish, New Kent County, but by 1721 was part of St. Paul's Parish, Hanover County. In 1747 David Thomson purchased 100 acres on Totopotomoy Creek from George Butler who had acquired the land through his wife, the former Elizabeth Wilkinson, a daughter of George Wilkinson. In 1758 John Thomson purchased one hundred four acres on the north side of Totopotomoy Creek from Joseph Crenshaw.[1] Processioners records for the parish note that in 1763 John Thomson replaced David Thomson as landowner. Presumably by 1765 Thomson had built a house on the property, for in that year he and his wife, the former Ann Garland, had a daughter named Susannah. In 1782 Susannah Thomson married Thomas Tinsley (1755-1822), a son of Thomas Tinsley (1731-1774) of Hanovertown.[2]

Susannah Thomson Tinsley's husband had been appointed by Governor Jefferson as Captain of the Hanover Militia in 1781. After the Revolution,

1   Both deeds were given to the Virginia Historical Society in 1972 by James Tinsley Moncure.

2   Birth, marriage and death dates are taken from Tinsley Family Bible records at the

Thomas continued to operate his family's tavern in Hanovertown. He and Nathaniel Anderson began a mercantile partnership in the town, a business that Tinsley continued to operate until 1796. Thomas was elected in 1786 to the vestry of St. Paul's Church and served as warden until the church closed its door about 1802. He was also elected to represent Hanover County in Virginia's House of Delegates in 1789 and was reelected to eight consecutive one-year terms. Tinsley served as Hanover County Sheriff, as chairman of the trustees of Washington-Henry Academy, was an active participant with other leading citizens in the Hanover Book Society, and was appointed Colonel of the 74th Virginia Light Infantry in 1794.

According to tax records for 1800, Colonel Tinsley purchased 400 acres from his mother-in-law, Ann Sydnor, who had remarried after Thomson's death and was widowed again by that year. Most likely the 32' x 32' core of the white frame house standing today was built in 1799. A one-story addition was constructed about 1820, and another large room was added about 1840. A large family cemetery was established a few hundred feet from house.

The Colonel's son, Thomas Garland Tinsley (1788-1859), inherited the house and property at the death of his mother in 1844. He and his first wife, the former Harriet Bryan (1803-1841) of York County, had one daughter, Harriet (1828-1903) who married Jacquelin Taliaferro, and three sons: Dr. Thomas Tinsley (1825-1873), Dr. Alexander Tinsley (1832-1911), and Seaton Tinsley (1836-1901) who married Fannie Gaines, daughter of Dr. William F. and Jane Spindle Gaines of Powhite, Hanover County.

Thomas Garland Tinsley and his second wife, the former Martha (Patsey) Rutherfoord (1803-1873) of Richmond, had one son, James Garland Tinsley (1843-1920) who inherited Totomoi. James married Martha (Pattie) Winston Jones Jones:Martha (Pattie) (Patty) Winston" (1843-1911), a daughter of Laney and Martha Ann Watt Jones of neighboring Hilly Farm. He and Pattie had one son and seven daughters. In 1921 ownership of Totomoi passed to their daughter, Clair Tinsley Jones (1873-1947), and at Clair's death to her sister Margaret's son, Thomas Rutherfoord Moncure (1911-2003). The property was placed on the National Register of Historic Places in 1976. In recent years Moncure's three daughters, who represent the seventh generation of family ownership, supervised a careful restoration of the old family home.

Walnut Lane. *Pamunkey Woman's Club Ccalendar,* March 1998, by Richard H. Jenkins.

Walnut Lane

This home is located on Cold Harbor Road, near Beaverdam Creek and the old Ellerson's Mill site. The land upon which this old house stands was once owned by Anthony Winston who in l769 deeded three parcels to John Austin: (1) "Old plantation" where Isaac Winston died 247-1/2 acres on White's Mill Pond; (2) 238-3/4 acres on Beaverdam Swamp, called Tarkiln Ridge; and (3) 59 acres low ground on Chickahominy Swamp granted to said Anthony Winston and John East about 1756. By 1782, John Austin was paying taxes on 800 acres and in 1801, 1,452 acres. In Glazebrook's *Hanover Migrations*, v. 2, p. 38, he gave a deposition, " . . . taken at his own house 27 August 1807 . . . that he was 80 years old on 14 September last." He died 12 December 1815, age about 88 years old.

In 1812, John Austin, Sr. for love and affection for his grandson, William Smith Austin, gave him all that tract of land "bought by me from Philip and William White . . . East by Capt. Macon's (Fairfield), South by Chickahominy Swamp, and West of William White and North of Nathan Bell." This early deed was "re-admitted" March 1866, "the records having been destroyed." William Smith Austin (ca. 1788-1866) married ca. 1811 Nancy Winn (ca. 1794-1849), daughter of John Winn and they made Walnut Lane their home for many years, until their deaths. Their tombstones are in the old bricked-in cemetery on the premises. In a Chancery suit, Sarah T. Sydnor, William S. Austin's daughter, became the next owner. She was the

137

wife of William B. Sydnor of Meadow Farm. She conveyed the property, consisting then of 197.4 acres to George K. Crutchfield in 1873, whose daughter, Maria, had married Thomas W. Sydnor of Mayfield, her son. There were other owners of this property after this date, until 1946 when George Wallace Bruce purchased Walnut Lane from George R. Tener, son of Katherine Tener, the previous owner, 197.4 acres.

Walnut Lane will be remembered by the many "box parties" and dances held in the large dining room during the Tener's occupancy. It will also be remembered as Bruce's Riding Academy. The young people of this area, as well as of Richmond, will remember the beautiful and gentle horses, the riding trails; as well as the parties given in the old barn.

The original home was three-story. Two rooms in the basement with center hall; first and second floors had two rooms also, one-room deep on each side of the center hall. The attic had walk-up steps, but was unfinished. The house is frame over a brick foundation. The basement steps are original as well as the wide beams. The home has been remodeled through the years. The front column were added by George Wallace Bruce after 1946.

[Note: Walnut Lane has been demolished. Bruce's Estates Subdivision now occupies the former homesite. The old home was located south of Route 156, within sight of Ellerson's Mill.]

Watt House or Springfield. *Pamunkey Woman's Club Calendar*, August 1988, by Janet Ogden Thomson.

Watt House or Springfield

This historic home, now a part of the Richmond Battlefield Tour, is believed to have been built about 1836 and is now used as the living quarters for personnel of the National Park Service, to provide protection and maintenance of the property.

This area was the scene of fierce fighting during the battle of Gaines' Mill which surged all over this farm in 1862. General Lee lost 8,000 men and McClellan lost over 6,000. Bullet holes the size of small apples could be seen in the weather boarding at one time. The house was the headquarters for General Fitz-John Porter and was also used as a hospital. A resident recalled Civil War Veterans who came on horseback once or twice a year to sit under the catalpa tree and reminisce in the early 1900's. It is amazing that this home still stands after going through such a conflict. A resident once said that it was able to withstand the elements because it was built with such good quality materials.

The house began showing signs of decay by 1935 when the Civilian Conservation Corps repaired it, and in 1958, the National Park Service began stabilization work, repairing the masonry, replacing window panes, painting, etc., and today we have this historic structure restored to its original appearance. At one time there was an old-fashioned carriage house and a two-room house on the property which have disappeared. The wide pine flooring on the upper floors is original.

The name originally was Springfield, but after the Civil War it was known as the Watt House, which was named after the family of Hugh Watt (1774-1850) and his wife, Sarah Bohannon Kidd (1784-1863). According to family knowledge, Springfield was once a part of Pitman Kidd's farm, whose daughter, Sarah Bohannon Kidd, married Hugh Watt in 1802. He was a native of Ireland. The Watt family and their descendants have contributed much to the history of Hanover County. One son, George Watt (1815-1884) invented the Watt plow. A daughter, Mary Austin Watt, born 1805, married in 1827, John Haw III of Oak Grove; another daughter, Margaret Mills Watt, born 1811, married Richardson Tyree Haw, John's brother. Richardson T. and John Haw were sons of John Haw of Haw's Shop (later called Studley), whose families have been some of Hanover County's leading citizens. The Hugh Watt family lived at Springfield for almost thirty years before the war. The battle of June 27, 1862, forced them to leave, never to return. Mrs. Watt, a widow of over 75 years and sick in bed at this time, was carried to Oak Grove, the home of her daughter, Mrs. John Haw, where she died in a few months.

Springfield descended to the heirs of George Watt. In one deed it was described as having two tracts: Springfield and Parsons. The latter, with 65 acres, was sold in 1902 to Cleora Martin, wife of Andrew G. Martin; in 1906 the heirs sold Springfield to Archer A. McGhee, 399-1/4 acres. Other owners were Dr. Frederick E. White of Canada, 1911; Minetree J. Fulton, 1917; and in 1928, 60 acres were sold to the Richmond Battlefield Parks, including the dwelling.

Waverly. Courtesy Hanover County Historical Society. Original photo by Bobbie Benton in *Old Homes of Hanover County, Virginia.*

Waverly

Waverly was located on Route 360 in what is now the business district of Mechanicsville, but in 1848 it was a plantation consisting of 221 acres. The house was two-story frame, over a brick basement, one room deep with side staircase in hall. When John S. Sledd purchased the house in 1911, there was a two-story log house in the rear joined to the main house by a breezeway. Two Norway Spruce trees were on each side of the yard, and the large depression in the front yard was a shell hole from the fighting around Mechanicsville during the Seven Days Battle. There were also bullet holes in the exterior of the house indicating it was in the line of fire during the Civil War. In Douglas S. Freeman's *Lee's Lieutenants*, v. 1, p. 514, "General Lee had ridden out and had posted himself in Binford's field, where, if anywhere, he could see what was happening." A confederate veteran told John S. Sledd, Sr. who was living at Waverly at the time of his visit, that General Lee barely escaped with his life at the site of the old carriage house which was to the rear of the home.

Waverly was once the home of Henry T. Drewery and Martha Amelia, his wife, later of Chesterfield County, who sold the property in 1848 to William A. Binford (ca. 1810). William A. Binford's wife was Lucy C., his second wife; his children were: Indiana by his first marriage; William J., Wirt M., and James E., by his second marriage. It was this Binford family who lived at Waverly during the Civil War and when General Robert E.

Lee posted himself in Binford's field. By 1876, William A. Binford was deceased and the property was in possession of his son, William J. Binford and Virginia N., his wife. After the Binford's ownership Richard A. Perrin and others owned the property of 130 acres, who sold it in 1897 to Jacob F. Acree. On 20 September 1911 a deed was given to John S. Sledd by Acree for the 130 acres. The family of John Sledd (1863-1941) and his wife, Neva W. (Lipscomb) Sledd (1872-1960) lived here for many years. After Mr. Sledd enlarged and remodeled the old home, it was two rooms deep on side and one room on the other with back porch and with a center hall. Waverly will also be remembered for its school for first graders, run by Mrs. Averil (Sledd) Chapel and her sister Mrs. Helena (Sledd) Shelton.

Waverly was still in the Sledd family when it was sold in the 1970's when highway 360 was fast becoming the business area of Mechanicsville. The house was destroyed and eventually a store was built on the site of the home tract, and other stores and businesses were constructed on the field where once General Lee had camped.

Williamsville. Photo by Leah Taylor.

Williamsville

Williamsville is named for its original owner, William Pollard, and was built by 1803, the date on the bricks over the front door. He lived here until his death in 1840. The records show that John Haw was its construction overseer and its contractor was Benjamin Ellett. Williamsville is located on Route 615, not far from Studley. William Pollard was clerk of Hanover County from 1781 to 1824, and succeeded his father, William Pollard (1726-1781) of Buckeye, which is located a few miles distant, and who was clerk of the court for forty-one years. William Pollard, the second, was born at Buckeye in 1760. His farm, Williamsville, consisted of over 1,000 acres. He married (1) in 1786 Elizabeth (Smelt) Dabney, widow of Isaac Dabney. They had two children, Mary Anderson Pollard, who married John Darracott, and Elizabeth Smelt Pollard, who married Dr. Joseph M. Sheppard; (2) Elizabeth (Dabney) Shackelford, widow of Lyn Shackleford, and daughter of George and Elizabeth Price Dabney. Their son, Dr. George William Pollard, born ca. 1814, inherited Williamsville and lived here until his death.

Dr. George William Pollard married Mary Peachey Todd of King & Queen County. The farm was then in its prime and was both beautiful and extensive, yielding large crops. Mrs. Pollard was a musician and gracious hostess. She laid out a beautiful flower garden, and the lovely boxwoods still abound at Williamsville. There was a lake just outside the garden with an island in it, and a bridge reached it from the mainland, surrounded by luxuriant shade trees and shrubbery.

During the Civil War, Williamsville was at one time the tenting ground of the enemy. Generals Grant, Hooker, and Meade took up headquarters in the house and farm.

This elegant home remained in the Pollard family until 1936. In 1964 Mr. and Mrs. R. W. Cabaniss purchased it, and have restored the mansion and surroundings to its original beauty.

PART FOUR

THE CENSUS

United States Census 1850

The year 1850 is a good midpoint or point of reference for the time period in these articles. This is especially timely because of the nature of the 1850 United States Census. This census was the first to provide specific information beyond the name of the head of the household.

Many families and individual family members are mentioned in the articles. In an effort to provide more insight into these times and characters, the families in which these characters can be clearly identified are listed this census section. This listing is limited to the 1850 census for Hanover County, Henrico County and Richmond.

It is interesting to note who was with whom, how many brothers and sisters there were, their ages, parents, occupation, the value of the real estate of the head of the household and others, and where each was born. In some cases, there is even an indication (*) that some were married within the year. The families listed have been copied from Joseph F. and Isobel B. Inman's *Hanover County, Virginia 1850 United States Census.* The Henrico County and City of Richmond families were abstracted from the Henrico County United States Census.

The Hanover County families were enumerated between 21 November 1850 and 14 December 1850. All persons listed in a given family were living there as of 1 June 1850.

Two changes were made to the Inman's original information. The letter "E" or "W" has been inserted after the "Family Number" and the house or plantation the family owned has been included in the "Value of Real Estate" column. The "E" represents the South Eastern Census District which was entirely within the old Saint Paul's Parish in eastern Hanover County. The "W" indicates the West Census District which was in the old Saint Martin's Parish and part of Saint Paul's Parish. Many of the families shown in the West Census District are typically associated with, geographically speaking, eastern Hanover County.

The dividing line between the parishes was from the point where Goochland, Hanover and Louisa county lines intersect, down Stone Horse Creek to the South Anna River, down the South Anna River to its confluence with North Anna River where the Pamunkey River forms.

The house or plantation, if known, is shown in bold text and is a cross-reference to the "Homes" section where there is further information consisting of articles from *Old Homes of Hanover County, Virginia.* There are several instances where the home is known, but no article is available.

No.	Name	Age	Sex	Occupation	Estate Value	Birth Place
74 E	**AUSTIN family of Walnut Lane**					
	William S.	61	M	Farmer	5,000	Va.
	WHITE					
	Charlotte	44	F			"
77 E	**BINFORD family of Waverly**					
	Wm. A.	30	M	Farmer	5,500	"
	Lucy A.	38	F			"
	Indiana	11	F			"
	William J.	4	M			"
	Wirt M.	3	M			"
	James E.	2	M			"
	KING					
	Robt.	35	M			"
764 W	**CHESTERMAN**					
	John T.	42	M	Farmer	1,700	"
	Mary F.	35	F			"
	Alonzo D.	10	M			"
	BUCHENEN					
	Richard	24	M	Laborer		"
85 E	**CURTIS family of Puccoon**					
	Henry	58	M	Physician		"
	CURTIS					
	Maria C.	26	F			"
	M. C.	20	F			"
	MUNFORD					
	Annie E.	28	F			"
	Robert	10	M			"
	Christiana	6	F			"

No.	Name	Age	Sex	Occupation	Estate Value	Birth Place
780 W	**DUNTON**					
	T. L.	36	M	Teacher		Vt.
	T. J.	36	F			Mass.
	T. J. T.	8	F			Va.
82 E	**ELLERSON family of Laurel Springs**					
	John H.	48	M	Farmer	10,000	Penn.
	Laura E.	30	F			Va.
	John H., Jr.	15	M			"
	Andrew R.	5	M			"
	Mary R.	1	F			"
131 E	**GAINES family of Powhite**					
	William F.	46	M	Farmer	30,000	"
	Jane E.	36	F			"
	Sallie G.	17	F			"
	Fanny W.	15	F			"
	CARLTON					
	Myra L.	48	F			
	Sally G.	18	F			"
	Ella C.	16	F			"
	Georgianna	14	F			"
	Juliet	12	F			"
	Alice	10	F			"
	George	8	M			"
839 W	**GARDNER family of Avondale**					
	Thomas	51	M	Farmer	11,000	"
	Sally M.	20	F			"
	James B.	17	M	Student		"
	Reuben	15	M			"
	Harriett N.	13	F			"
	Mary E.	5	F			"
*_W	**HAW family of Oak Grove**					
	John	48	M	Machinist	4,500	"
	Mary A.	45	F			"
	Sarah E.	17	F			"

No.	Name	Age	Sex	Occupation	Estate Value	Birth Place
	HAW (continued from previous page)					
	Mary J.	15	F			Va.
	John H.	12	M			"
	George P.	12	M			"
	William	10	M			"
	Edwin	7	M			"
	Joseph R.	5	M			"
*_W	DAVENPORT					
	Isaac	22	M	Machinist		"
*_W	CROSS					
	Charles P.	21	M	Machinist		"
*_W	GRAVES					
	George W.	19	M	Machinist		"
	COOK					
	William	15	M			"
	WATT					
	Cornelia M.	6	F			"
799 W	**HAW family of Locust Hill**					
	Margaret M.[1]	39	F		2,500	"
	Sally C.	17	F			
	Margaret A.	15	F			"
	Mary E.	13	F			"
	Richardson W.	12	M			"
	Harriet A.	10	F			"
	Cornelia N.	7	F			"
	Helen M.	5	F			"
	Rosaline W.	3	F			"
	Osborne J.	1	M			"

---

1   R[ichardson]. T. Haw, husband of Margaret, d. Aug 1849, b. Va., Farmer.

No.	Name	Age	Sex	Occupation	Estate Value	Birth Place
76 E	**HOOPER family of Beaverdam Farm**					
	Joseph	42	M			Va.
	Elizabeth C.	43	F			"
	Sarah H.	18	F			"
	Thomas W.	17	M			"
	Pauline	12	F			"
	Mary Ann	10	F			"
	Wm. D.	8	M			"
	Elizabeth	6	F			"
	LYLE					
	Elizabeth	55	F			"
	HUDSON					
	Richard	18	M			"
	ARGYLE					
	Edward	19	M			"
	CLARK					
	Thomas	18	M			"
	KING					
	Wesley	18	M			"
	ACREE					
	David	17	M			"
	HUDSON					
	Wm. B.	23	M			"
	WHITLOCK					
	Francis J.	35	M			"
762 W	**LUMPKIN**					
	Archiles	50	M	Farmer	8,000	"
	Nancy	51	F			"
	John G.	19	M	Student		"
	Judith	18	F			"

151

No.	Name	Age	Sex	Occupation	Estate Value	Birth Place

830 W POLLARD family of Williamsville

	Name	Age	Sex	Occupation	Estate Value	Birth Place
	Geo. W.	36	M	Physician		Va.
	Mary P.	31	F			"
	Bernard C.	12	M			"
	Ellen E.	9	F			".
	Wm.	8	M			"
	Elizabeth P.	70	F			"

SMITH
| | Richard | 35 | M | Overseer | | " |

831 W POLLARD family of Buckeye

	Name	Age	Sex	Occupation	Estate Value	Birth Place
	William T. H.	39	M	Farmer	3,800	"
	Susan C.	38	F			"
	Molly T.	12	F			"
	Betsy B.	9	F			"
	Willianna	5	F			"
	Alice	3	F			"
	Maria L.	5 mo.	F			"

OSBORNE
| | Henry L. | 29 | M | Preacher, Pres. | | S.C. |

CONVERSE
| | Abigail | 35 | F | | | N.H. |

1044 W PRICE family of Dundee

	Name	Age	Sex	Occupation	Estate Value	Birth Place
	L. B.	40	M	Farmer	23,000	Va.
	Ellen M.	37	F			"
	Eliza W.	7	F			"
	Ann O.	5	F			"
	L. B.	3	M			"
	James W.	35	M	Farmer		"

805 W RUFFIN family of Marlbourne

	Name	Age	Sex	Occupation	Estate Value	Birth Place
	Edmund	56	M	Farmer	37,100	".
	Rebecca	27	F			"
	Elizabeth	26	F			"

No.	Name	Age	Sex	Occupation	Estate Value	Birth Place
	RUFFIN (continued from previous page)					
	Mildred	23	F			Va.
	Jane	21	F			"
	Ella	17	F			"
838 W	**SHELTON family of Rural Plains**					
	Edwin	50	M	Farmer	10,000	"
	Sarah E.	39	F			"
	Harriett A.	21	F			"
	Mary E.	19	F			"
	Frances F.	17	F			"
	Edwin T.	14	M			"
	Sarah E.	13	F			"
	Emma E.	7	F			"
	Walter M.	1 mo.	M			"
339 W	**STARKE**					
	Jos.	51	M	Farmer	1,800	"
	M. T.	51	F			"
	HARWOOD					
	G. B.	24	M			"
	STARKE					
	R.W.	21	M	Physician		"
	John K.	15	M	Student		"
	Susan	70	F			"
	Josephine	1	F			"
73 E	**SYDNOR family of Meadow Farm**					
	Wm. B.	44	M	Farmer	9,000	"
	Sarah J.	38	F			"
	Wm. J.	20	M	Surveyor		"
	Sarah B.	18	F			"
	Edward G.	16	M	Brick Maker		"
	Anne E.	15	F			"
	Thomas W.	13	M			"

No.	Name	Age	Sex	Occupation	Estate Value	Birth Place
SYDNOR (continued from previous page)						
	Mary W.	11	F			Va.
	John L.	10	M			"
	George B.	8	M			"
	Julia C.	6	F			"
	Robt. T.	4	M			"
	Walter	3	M			"
	Charles	1	M			"
	NASH					
	Ebenezer	26	M	Wheelwright		N.Y
	GUNN					
	Elisha G.	23	M	Teacher		Va.
788 W	**TALLEY**					
	John	62	M	Farmer	2,500	"
	Sarah B.	61	F			"
	Thomas W.	28	M			"
	Nat H. *	26	M			"
	Mary J.*	17	F			"
	Lucy W.	24	F			"
	Sarah M.	24	F			"
864 W	**TINSLEY family of Totomoi**					
	Thomas G.	61	M	Farmer	30,000	"
	Patsey	46	F			"
	Alexander	17	M	Student		"
	Seaton	14	M			"
	James	7	M			"
140 E	**WATT family of Watt House/Springfield Farm**					
	Sarah B.[2]	65	F		7,000	"
	Hugh	75	M			Ire.
	George	3	M			Va.

* marred within the year

2   Sarah is probably listed as head of household as she inherited the land from her father, Pitman Kidd.

No.	Name	Age	Sex	Occupation	Estate Value	Birth Place

WATT (continued from previous page)

| | Pitman K. | 42 | M | | | Va. |

1062 W WINSTON

	Wm. D.	58	M	Lawyer	10,000	"
	Elizabeth S.	47	F			"
	Ann F.	21	F			"

TAYLOR

	Jno. R.	24	M	Merchant	8,000	"
	Sallie E.	19	F			"
	Wm. D.	17	M	Student		"

CALLIS

| | Tobias L. | 50 | M | School Master | | " |

1045 W WINSTON family at Courtland

	Wm. O.	37	M	County Clk.	9,000	"
	Sarah A.	26	F			"
	Phillip B.	4	M			"
	Betty B.	6	F			"
	Sally M.	3	F			"
	Fendal G.	1	M			"

150 E WOODY family of Pointer's or David Woody's

	David	48	M	Farmer	2,000	"
	Mary	44	F			"
	Elisha	15	M			"
	Charles D.	13	M			"
	Mary A. E.	10	F			"
	Christianna B.	7	F			"

155

No.	Name	Age	Sex	Occupation	Estate Value	Birth Place

The following individuals lived in the City of of Richmond which was considered Henrico County in 1850.

660 R* WATT, Jr.

	Name	Age	Sex	Occupation	Estate Value	Birth Place
	George	25	M	Plough Maker		Va.

SUMMER

	Name	Age	Sex	Occupation	Estate Value	Birth Place
	William S.	31	M	Machinist	750	Mass.

5 H* WHITE

	Name	Age	Sex	Occupation	Estate Value	Birth Place
	Phillip B.[1]	38	M	Merchant	2,500	Va.
	Elizabeth A.	40	F			"
	Mary L.	16	F			"
	Thos. W.	14	M			"
	Harriett E.	12	F			"
	Wm. S.	10	M			"

* "H" denotes living in Henrico. "R" denotes living in Richmond.

---

1   Phillip B. White was born at Beaverdam Farm.

BIBLIOGRAPHY

Brock, Robert Alonzo, editor. *Southern Historical Society Papers.* Volume 39, Richmond, VA: Southern Virginia Historical Society, 1914.

Chamberlayne, C. G., editor. *The Vestry Book of St. Paul's Parish Hanover County, Virginia 1706 – 1786.* Richmond, VA: Virginia State Library & Archives, 1940.

Cocke, III, William Ronald. *Hanover County Chancery Wills and Notes.* Baltimore, MD: Genealogical Publishing, Co., Inc., 1978.

_____. *Hanover County Taxpayers Saint Paul's Parish 1782 – 1815.* Columbia, MD: William Ronald Cocke, 1956.

Fisher, Carl W. *Zeta At Historic Hampden-Sydney, 1850-1912.* Germantown, MD: 1939.

Gabbert, John M., *Military Operations in Hanover County, Virginia 1861 – 1865,* Roanoke, VA: John M Gabbert, 1989.

Glazebrook, Eugenia G. and Preston G., eds, *Virginia Migrations: Hanover County,(1723-1850) Wills, Deeds Depositions, Invoices, Letters and Other Documents of Historical and Genealogical Interest,* Genealogical Publishing Company, Richmond, VA: 1949.

Hanover County Historical Society Bulletin, Volume I, 1969 -1987. Hanover, VA, *Hanover County Historical Society,* no date.

_____. *Hanover County Historical Society Bulletin, Volume II 1987 -2002.,* 2007.

_____. *Old Homes of Hanover County, Virginia.* Salem, VA: Walsworth Publishing Company, 1983.

Haw, M. J. "My Visits to Grandmother." *Christian Observer, Volume 9,* Louisville, KY: May 18, 1910.
_____. *Diary of M. J. Haw, unpublished, no date.*

Haw, Joseph R. "Haw's Shop Community of Virginia." *Confederate Veteran* Magazine, *Volume 33*, Nashville, TN: 1925.

_____. "The Battle of Haw's Shop, Va." *Confederate Veteran Magazine, Volume 33*, Nashville, TN: 1925.

_____. "Haw Boys in the War Between the States." *Confederate Veteran Magazine, Volume 33*, Nashville, TN: 1925.

_____."Captain Joseph R. Haw"*Confederate Veteran, Vol. XXXVI #1*, January 1926.

Hill, General D. H. "The Battle of Gaines's Mill." <u>*The Century Illustrated Monthly Magazine, 30*</u>, New York: The Century Co., 1882-1913.

Hooper, Thomas W. "About Beaverdam." *Richmond Dispatch,* February 2, 1895.
_____. "Those Good Old Days." *Richmond Dispatch*, February 10, 1895.
_____. "Pole Green Church." *Richmond Dispatch*, March 3, 1895.
_____. "Hanover Memories." *Richmond Dispatch*, March 10, 1895.
_____. "Old Time Politics." *Richmond Dispatch*, March 31, 1895.
_____. "Old Beulah Church." *Richmond Dispatch*, April 7, 1895.

Inman, Joseph F. and Isobel, *Hanover County Virginia Census, 1850*, self-published, Richmond VA: 1998.

Lancaster, Robert Bolling. *A Sketch of the Early History of Hanover County Virginia and Its Large and Important Contributions to the American Revolution.* Richmond, VA: Whittet & Sheppardson, 1976.

Lowry, Judith P. & Patricia A. Baber. *Hanover County, Virginia Death Register 1853–1896*. Montpelier, VA: Page Library of Local History & Genealogy, 2006.

Manarin, Louis H., *15th Virginia Infantry*. Lynchburg: H. Howard, Inc., 1990.

Pamunkey Woman's Club Calendars, 1985-2017, custodial digital images, Hanover County Historical Society Archives and Special Collections.

Pippenger, Wesley E., compiler. *Death Notices from Richmond, Virginia Newspapers 1841-1853*. Richmond, VA: Genealogical Society, 2002.

Virginia Genealogical Society. *Marriages and Deaths from Richmond, Virginia Newspapers 1780-1820.* Special Publication No. 8. Richmond, VA: Virginia Genealogical Society, 1983.

Wallace, Jr., Lee A. *A Guide to Virginia Military Organizations 1861 – 1865.* Lynchburg, VA: H. E. Howard, Inc., 1986.

_____. *The Richmond Howitzers.* Lynchburg, VA: H. E. Howard, Inc., 1993.

Index

Made in the USA
Coppell, TX
01 September 2020